R06876

KV-413-909

College Library Medway College of Design

WITHDRAWN FROM STOCK

D116638

SPRANG

Thread Twisting, A Creative Textile Technique

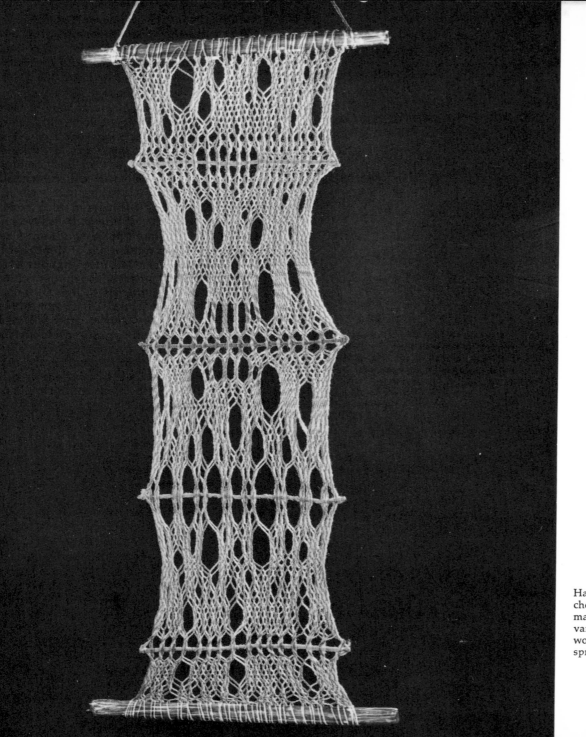

Hanging, cotton and
chenille, Kit Chap-
man. An interesting
variety of openings is
worked through this
sprang.

SPRANG

Thread Twisting, A Creative Textile Technique

Hella Skowronski & Mary Reddy

14423

746·4224
Sko

STUDIO VISTA

Acknowledgments

The joy of our endeavor has been not only the work itself but the people with whom we have worked. It was gratifying to find so many people who gave so freely of their time and talents. Special thanks to:

Lisa Ridenour, illustrator, who put our words into visual form with such clarity and simplicity.

William Eng, photographer, who so ably captured the beauty and essence of sprang.

Jean Wilson, author of several books on weaving, who offered advice on writing and planning a book. Her help made the task so much easier.

The students of Hella Skowronski, whose talents and ingenuity are evident in many of the photographs in this book. They can be an inspiration to any beginner in sprang.

Doris Brockway, Associate Professor, School of Home Economics, University of Washington, Seattle, Elsbeth Pfenninger, and Claudia Tarlyn, who so willingly offered their assistance.

Mary Reddy's husband Jim, who, with kindness and consideration, put up with a part-time wife for so long.

Studio Vista
Cassell & Collier Macmillan Publishers Limited, London
35 Red Lion Square, London WC1R 4SG
Sydney, Auckland, Toronto, Johannesburg

© 1974 Litton Educational Publishing, Inc.
All rights reserved. No part of this publication may be reproduced, stored in a retrieval system, or transmitted, in any form or by any means, electronic, mechanical, photocopying, recording or otherwise, without the prior permission of Studio Vista

All photographs are by William Eng, unless otherwise credited
All diagrams are by Lisa Ridenour
Loom shown on page 13 courtesy of The Loomery

First published in the United States by
Van Nostrand Reinhold Company 1974
First published in Great Britain by Studio Vista 1974

ISBN 0-289-70460-x

Opposite
Hanging, wool, Claudia Tarlyn. A mixture of twists and yarns creates interesting patterns.

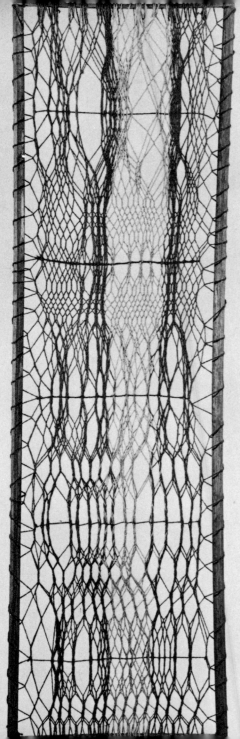

Contents

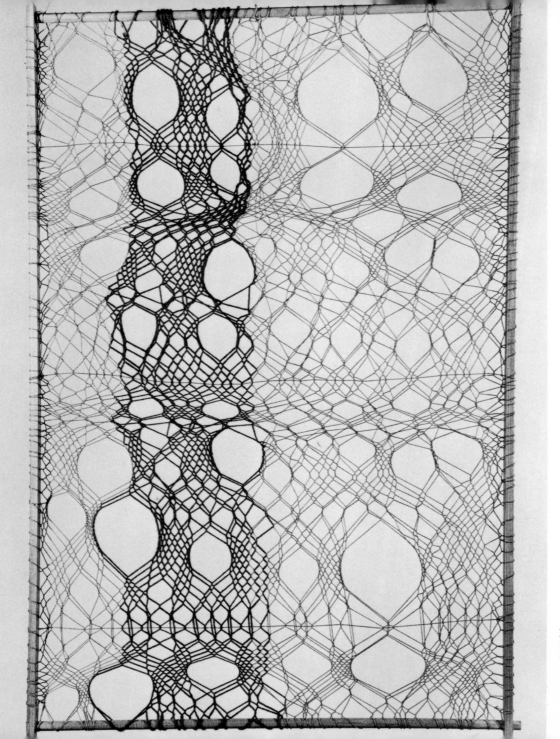

Hanging, cotton, Marney Chapman. A mixture of twists in fine and heavy yarn creates a complex sprang structure.

Introduction

Sprang is a delightful discovery, one that offers almost unlimited possibilities in color, design, and use. Sprang may be your medium for making decorative hangings or useful articles for yourself and friends. It may be a new form of expanding and releasing your imagination. It may become your path to some extra pocket money. Whatever your reasons for learning a handcraft, sprang is sure to fit the bill—get ready to become the master of a new and rewarding craft.

The word sprang may be new to you. Actually, both the name, derived from an ancient Swedish word, and the craft itself are very old indeed. Bronze Age fragments, found in Danish and Norwegian peat bogs dating from 1500—1100 B.C., appear to be caps, hairnets, and stockings. In Egyptian graves of the Coptic period, about the 4th and 5th century A.D. and later, there have been found sprang-like capes, bags with drawstrings, lacy and woolen pieces that might have been scarves, and other articles. Analysis of the method by which these were made shows it to be similar to sprang, and many features of our modern craft—delicate patterns of slits, looped closings, changed direction of twists—are evident. The term Egyptian plaiting comes from these pieces, and is a name sometimes given to sprang, although the Egyptian textiles themselves have often been called net, lace, or *filet de dentelle*.

No one knows where sprang originated. Evidence of an early version of sprang was located in excavations of an ancient culture in Peru. Paintings on early Greek vases depict women making a fabric very similar in appearance to sprang. In our own times, sprang has been in common use in Czechoslovakia, in Mexico, where it is used for shopping bags and hammocks, and among the Winnebago Indians of Wisconsin, who used it to make woolen scarves. At various times sprang has been used in Syria, Persia, Tunisia, Eastern Europe, and Scandanavia. Military sashes in a diagonal sprang pattern were very popular around the end of the eighteenth and beginning of the nineteenth century in Denmark, Germany, and France, and had to be imported into Canada after the French arrival. As you can see, sprang has not only made its way through the centuries but also around the world.

This craft, which is so old and yet so brand new, is, very simply, a network of threads twisted over each other. When finished, the simplest kind of sprang looks like a net or mesh. As in weaving the threads are first placed onto a loom, one that you can make yourself. Then, starting from the bottom of the loom, rows of twists are made. What is unique about sprang is that each row of twists made at the bottom of the frame is automatically formed at the top also. The top mirrors the bottom of the piece, with the two halves meeting in the center.

When you remove your first piece from the loom, and even as you are working, you will discover the true nature of sprang—it's springy! In fact, a word of warning at this point. Do not despair if sometimes your sprang relaxes into a formless mass when you remove it from the loom. Once shaped and blocked or perhaps framed, your sprang will become the beautiful work you intended it to be.

The elastic nature of sprang is, in fact, a very positive factor. In early days, sprang was used for bonnets and night caps because it formed to the head. It is useful today in many kinds of clothing, whether you want a form-fitting article or not.

Let the springiness of sprang work for you. Stretch and coax your work into any number of shapes. It does not have to be a rigid square or rectangle. Half of the fun of sprang can be in finding the infinite possibilities of a finished piece.

Because sprang is a rediscovery, a reborn craft, there was much to relearn and much to develop anew. Sprang still has room to grow, and you may be the one to find a new technique or a better method. As you learn this craft, you may also be helping to recreate it.

Even the vocabulary of sprang had to be developed, as the craft has never been indigenous to an English-speaking people, and very little has been written about it. Therefore, the terms used in this book are for the most part new. Sprang is sometimes spoken of as intertwining or plaiting. However, this book refers to the structure of sprang as twisting, as this is simpler and more direct. We hope you will find all of the terms we use both simple and descriptive.

As far as we know, some of the techniques in the book are wholly new creations, never used by ancient peoples or other modern craftsmen. These new techniques, such as applying continuous warp to sprang and spranging in sections, provide a broader scope for sprang than has ever been possible. Previously, sprang was limited in size by the size of the frame loom. This is no longer the case. Continuous warp, an established weaving method, can be used in combination with our new technique of spranging in sections to make pieces quite long. This allows you to sprang large hangings, ponchos, table runners, and more. Spranging in sections also makes it possible to work a number of different designs in the same piece.

Another exciting new technique which, at this writing, has never been previously published, will be of great interest to those of you who weave. A combination of weaving and sprang can be done in the same work on a weaving loom. The woven portions and the sprang are all of the same fabric. See Chapter 15 for some lovely examples.

Discover sprang for yourself. The intricacy of its structure, the many possibilities of its designs and uses, and the texture and color of the yarns all will play a role in making sprang a richly satisfying experience for you.

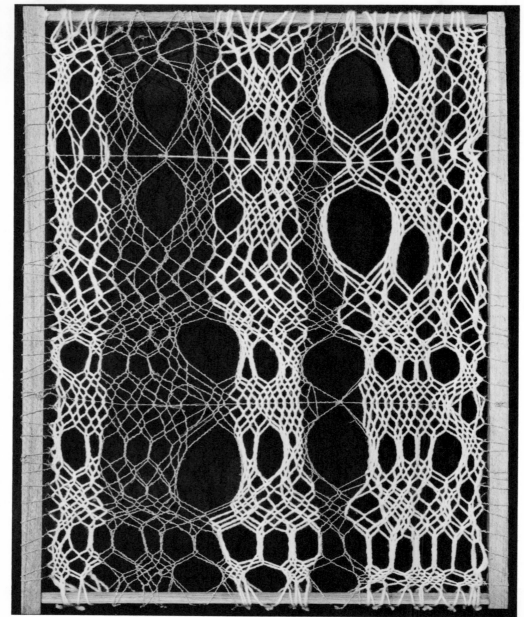

Hanging, wool and natural linen bouclé, Marney Chapman. A liberal use of openings, or slits, makes a visually active piece.

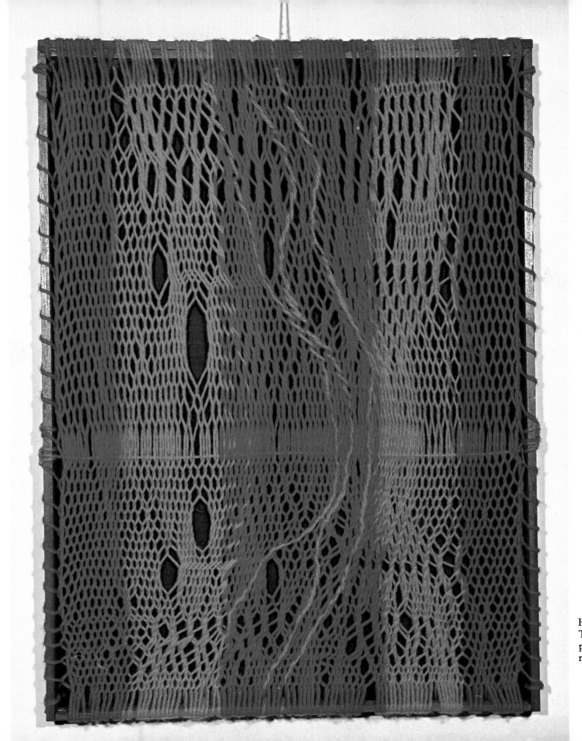

Hanging, knitting worsted, Hella Skowronski. The stripes and colors of this hanging on a permanent frame are unified by the flowing motion of the stitchery through the center.

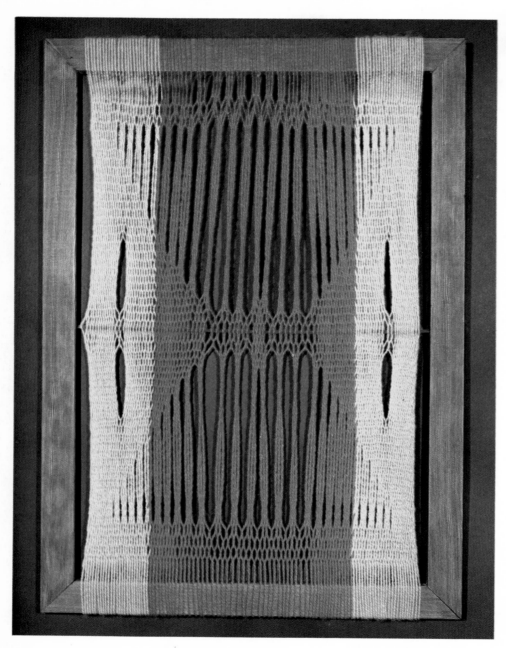

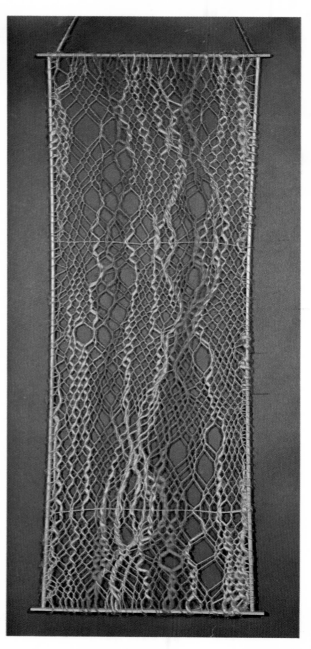

Hanging, yarn, Lyn Lambert. Top and bottom of columns are in trebles, the center is held together only by the fuzzy quality of the yarn.

Hanging, yarn, Aves Pickering. Uneven yarn and random distribution of openings change originally straight stripes into serpentines of color.

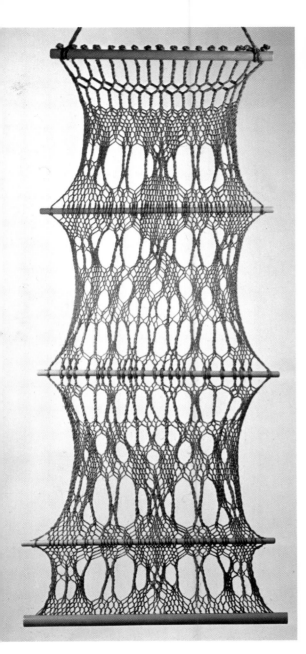

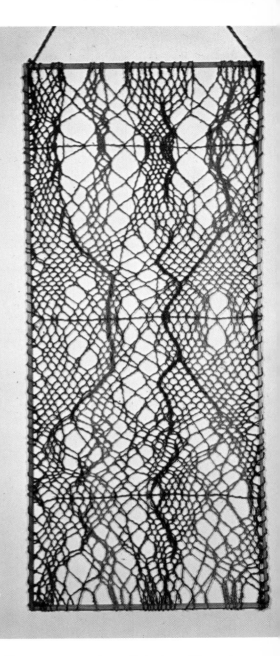

Hanging, heavy jute, Hella Skowronski. The same trebles are twisted, joined, and then separated again.

Hanging, slub rayon, heavy chenille, cotton suede, Mary Reddy. The shape of this hanging was created by warping on a number of dowels at different heights.

Hanging, yarn, Aves Pickering. The color stripes are distorted because of the blend of singles and slits. The heavy fluid lines are trebles.

11

Scarf, bulky wool, Mary Reddy. The pattern is produced by a closely set warp of alternating colors spranged with full twists.

Three-dimensional mask, Thai jute, Dorothy Tow. Large slits form the eyes of this primitive-looking mask spranged in red and purple.

Bright Angel, cape of leather and yarn, Luana Sever. The flexible nature of sprang is employed to its best advantage.

Three-dimensional hanging, yarn, Hella Skowronski. Full advantage is taken of the tendency of sprang to turn when the direction of the twist changes. The blue inner hanging was spranged separately.

1 Materials

Fig. 1-1. Sprang materials are inexpensive and easy to obtain. You will need a frame of some sort. It can be a simple picture frame. You can purchase a frame loom with an adjustable tension bar (A); or canvas stretchers to put together yourself (B). You will also need dowels (C); shed and transfer sticks (D); short pick-up stick (E); center cord for warping (F); shed cords (G); twine (H) or yarn (I); or any other appropriate warping material.

The craftsman, his equipment, and what he makes are inseparable parts of a total process. The finished work is perhaps the most exciting part—there's nothing like that feeling of accomplishment after you have made something really beautiful—but you, as the craftsman, are the most important part of that process. The more intimate the craftsman becomes with his equipment, the more he will appreciate both himself, as the maker, and the finished work he has made. Constructing your own equipment can only bring you closer to this feeling.

Sprang equipment consists of a few pieces of wood, yarn, cord, and a bit of miscellaneous paraphernalia, as shown in Figure 1–1. Of course, one of the most important components will be your own ideas. They may come from what you see around you—magazine pictures, landscapes, a small patch of earth and rock in your back yard. Perhaps you might work the environment right into your sprang in the form of found objects from the beach or woods. Or perhaps you are a craftsman who discovers ideas as you work with the yarn, deciding what is good and developing that. However your imagination works, give your ideas free play.

THE LOOM

The most necessary piece of equipment, shown in Figure 1-1, is the frame loom (A). This type of loom is simple to make and use, inexpensive and portable. Any square or rectangular frame, such as a picture frame, can be used.

The best type to begin with is one made from canvas stretchers (B), with inside dimensions of about 24″ x 36″. Canvas stretchers are made out of wood and come in four separate pieces that are easily assembled into a square or rectangle by interlocking the corners. Different lengths can be interchanged to make frames of varying sizes. Canvas stretchers can be bought at art supply or hardware stores and when assembled make a solid frame.

OTHER EQUIPMENT

DOWELS. Cut two ½″-diameter pieces, long enough to just clear the inside width of the frame (C). Sand well. You can buy dowels at a hardware store or lumber yard. The threads to be spranged will be wound between the dowels.

TWINE OR CORD. This should be strong enough not to break but flexible enough to knot easily (H). It is used to attach the dowels to the frame.

LONG STICKS. These are lengths of wood, about 1″ wide and ¼″ thick, and equal in length to the outside width of the frame (D). The ends are shaped and sanded to a rounded point. Then they are used as shed and transfer sticks while you are spranging. Buy two at a weaving supply store, where they are called pick-up sticks, or make your own from long rulers, such as can be found in paint stores. The sticks hold the sprang in place as it is being worked.

SHORT PICK-UP STICK. File one end of an ice-cream stick to a smooth point. The short stick is used to pick up the threads (E). Some people prefer to pick up the threads with their fingers. Try both methods to see which is best for you.

SHED CORDS. Cut six to eight pieces of thick, smooth cord, a little longer than the width of the frame (G). Cut one length of cord of a different color, long enough to tie across the width and to both sides of the frame (F). Parachute, drapery, upholstery, or macramé cord is suitable. Like the long pick-up sticks, the cord is used to hold the sprang in place while it is being worked.

STRETCH CORDS. Almost any piece of strong yarn or string can be used. As you work, these cords are tied through the edge of the sprang and to the sides of the frame to keep the sprang from drawing in.

SCISSORS. For general snipping when setting up or finishing.

TAPESTRY NEEDLE. This should be about 2" to 3" long with a dull point. It is used when spranging the closing row, the row that secures the whole piece so it does not unravel.

MASKING TAPE. The tape holds the threads at tension and in order as they are being wound onto the frame.

YARN. Choosing yarn is an enjoyable excursion into the world of color and texture. You may certainly begin by using up left-over balls of yarn around the house. If you are fortunate enough to have such a place in your town, browsing through a weaving supply store is a delight in itself. The variety of yarns is boundless—soft, rough, bright, muted, bulky, thin. No matter what you want to do with your sprang, you should be able to find a yarn to fit the bill. Don't be surprised if you become hooked on the beauty and variety of yarn—you won't be the first.

Weaving supply stores are not the only places to find yarns. Look in knitting and craft shops and macramé supply stores. Even hardware stores offer very usable twines and strings. Your resources are really endless.

Use smooth, heavy yarns at first. Jute, linen, bulky wool, heavy string, or twine make good choices. Macramé cord is also very workable.

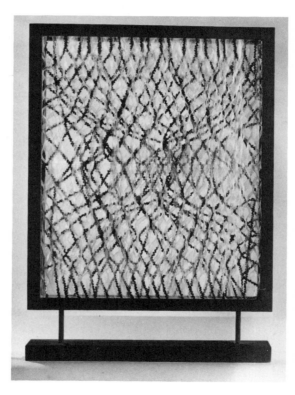

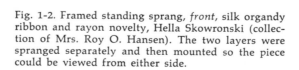

Fig. 1-2. Framed standing sprang, *front*, silk organdy ribbon and rayon novelty, Hella Skowronski (collection of Mrs. Roy O. Hansen). The two layers were spranged separately and then mounted so the piece could be viewed from either side.

Fig. 1-3. Framed standing sprang, *back*.

14

2 Set-Up and Warping

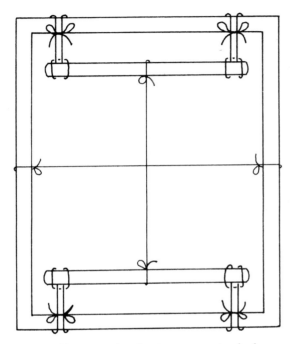

Fig. 2-1. Your completed set-up on a simple frame loom will look like this.

With some minor additions to your frame it can indeed be called a loom. Then the yarn will be wound onto it, ready for spranging. After setting up your loom once or twice, the process will be automatic and will take no longer than a few minutes.

The set-up described below is for a simple frame loom, on which you will no doubt do most of your work. However, there are other

loom possibilities. One of these is the permanent frame loom, used for wall hangings. The loom is called permanent because it actually becomes the frame for the hanging. More care must be given to the construction of a permanent frame loom but there is then no need to make a frame for the hanging after the hanging is completed. Complete instructions for warping and finishing a permanent frame are given in Chapter 14.

Sprang can also be done on a weaving loom. As far as we know, this is the first time such a technique has been presented. As mentioned previously, the length of a sprang piece is limited by the size of the frame. The weaving loom not only allows for longer and wider pieces but also variations of sprang in combination with weaving. Continuous warp, done on a frame loom as described in Chapter 3, provides for a larger piece also, although not as long as on a weaving loom. The larger the frame, the larger your work can be.

SETTING UP THE FRAME

1. Attach one dowel to the frame in the following manner. Cut two pieces of twine or strong string, each about 40″ long. Tie one piece of twine to one end of the dowel with a hitch (figs. 2–2 and 2–3). Tie the second string to the other end of the dowel in the same way.

2. Loop the free ends of the twine over the top, around the back and out the front of the frame. Bring these free ends around the twine supporting the dowel on the front of the frame. Tie a knot and bow (fig. 2–4).

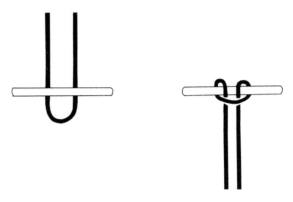

Fig. 2-2. To begin the hitch, loop the twine and place it behind the dowel, with the free ends up.

Fig. 2-3. To finish the hitch, bring the free ends in front of the dowel and through the loop.

Fig. 2-4. Tying the cord that comes from the top dowel and goes to the top of the frame.

3. Cut two more pieces of twine and attach the second dowel to the bottom of the frame in the same way. Leave room between the dowels and the frame for the ball of yarn to pass through.

As the piece is spranged, the tension on the yarn will become greater. The knotted lengths of twine, called tension-release cords, can be retied to loosen the tension. It is handiest to always loosen the tension-release cords holding the lower dowel.

4. Tie the dowels together in the middle to keep them stable. This cord can be removed after some yarn has been wound onto the dowels.

5. Adjust the dowels so they are parallel with the top and bottom of the frame.

6. Place the long center warping cord across the center of the frame, parallel with the dowels, and tie it to the sides of the frame.

Does your frame look like the one pictured in Figure 2–1? If it does, you've just set up a loom, and you are ready for work.

WARPING

The threads you will put on the loom are called the warp. Except for one thread, the closing, that will eventually be used in the last row spranged, no other threads need to be used. It is the warp threads, twisted over each other, that form the structure of the sprang. How you twist them determines the design of your sprang. The process of winding the yarn onto the loom is warping.

Warping is more than simply a way to put the threads in working order. It can be a very relaxing and satisfying process. Since the steps are not difficult to learn, you should be at ease with the motion of warping after little practice. You will also find that making the warp can be an integral and very important part of your new craft. As you combine different colors, textures, and sizes of yarn so that the warp complements the structural quality of the twists, you will see how the warp you have made will enhance and enliven your work.

Warp calculation

There are two points to consider in warp calculation, take-up and drawing-in. Due to the twisting of the threads, warp length shortens. This is called take-up. Also, a certain amount of shortening occurs when the finished piece has been steamed. For example, a 20″-long warp may block out as a finished piece to only 18″. The take-up in this case is 2″. You will find that some yarns have more take-up than others. It is generally safe to assume that 10–15% of the total warp length calculated will go to take-up.

Because of the elastic nature of the twists, the sides of the piece curve in toward the center. This is called drawing-in. Drawing-in does not effect the blocked measurement of the finished piece as much as take-up. A warp 10″ wide may block out to 9½″.

Determining approximately how much yarn you will need in your warp is a simple task. First, decide how long the finished work is to be. Then, each warp thread must be as long as the finished work, plus enough to allow for take-up. Always measure from the top of the top dowel to the bottom of the bottom dowel. This allows for the amount of yarn it takes to go around the dowels.

It is difficult to give absolutely precise rules for measuring the amount of yarn needed for one warp thread, and therefore for the total warp. Various factors come into play. First, a tight twist takes up more yarn than a loose twist. Second, a twist using four threads draws in and takes up more than a twist using two threads, and third, one type of yarn will take up and draw in more than another type of yarn. The best rule is that of experience.

After determining how long each warp thread is to be, for example, 20″, calculate the total number of warp threads. This figure is arrived at by multiplying the number of threads per inch by the number of inches in the width. For example, you may set your warp at 6 threads to the inch and the total warp at 10″ wide. You would multiply 6 threads × 10″ for a total of 60 threads. Once you have determined the number of threads, be sure not to cut the warp into that many pieces. The warp is actually only one long thread, wrapped around the dowels numerous times.

After you have found out how long each warp thread is and how many warp threads there are, simply multiply one figure by the other. Add in the amount of yarn needed to tie onto the dowels where the warp begins and again where it ends. Where you tie on and off, you will leave a long, dangling thread, approximately four to five times the length of the warp. All of this may or may not be used to finish the piece.

Here is an example. If one warp thread is 20″ long and you are warping 60 threads, the basic warp is 20″ × 60 threads = 1200″. Add 80–100″ for the extra lengths of thread used to tie onto the dowel at the beginning of the warp and to tie off at the end of the warp. This brings the total amount of yarn required to about 1296″ or 36 yards.

You will get a feel for how long and how wide to make your warp after you have worked with different twists and yarns.

Warping procedure

Before warping, mark the dowels every inch. These marks are used to indicate how many threads per inch are in your warp.

To begin, tie the yarn to the left side of the top dowel, using a knot and slipknot (figs.

2–5 and 2–6). Leave a long, dangling thread, about the length of four warp threads. This may be used in the finishing of the sprang if, for example, the sides must be lashed together. The warp is always started at the top so the slipknot and long thread are out of the working area.

To warp, follow the pattern shown in Figures 2–7 and 2–8. Here is the sequence of warping:

Bring the yarn under the center cord, under and over the lower dowel, over the center cord, under and over the top dowel, and repeat.

The center cord helps to keep the warp threads in sequence. It is then easier to adjust the tension of each thread, as it is kept separate from its neighbors.

Fig. 2-7. Cross section of figure-eight warp.

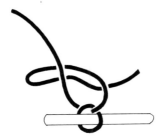

Fig. 2-5. Tying the slipknot that will begin your warp. First knot the twine around the dowel, and make a loop with the free end.

Fig. 2-6. To finish the slipknot, bring the loop around the other end and through the opening. Pull tight. Another slipknot is made when the warping is finished.

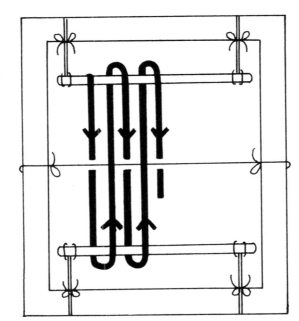

Fig. 2-8. Direction of warping. After a little practice, warping becomes a rhythmical and relaxing task.

Remember three points, and you will find warping trouble free.

1. The yarn always goes under and over the dowels.

2. The yarn from the top dowel goes under the cord.

3. The yarn from the lower dowel goes over the cord.

Finishing touches on the set-up

It is very important that all of the warp threads have the same tension, equally tight and not sagging. Adjust the tension about every ten loops around the dowels by pulling the threads on the top of the bottom dowel towards the top of the frame. Space the warp evenly over the inch marks on the dowels. With masking tape, secure the adjusted threads to the dowels. Be sure the warp threads are straight so the tension is even.

Make this first warp 40 threads wide. Determine the number of threads by counting the loops on the bottom dowel. One loop equals two threads, so you should have 20 loops in your first warp. You will use this warp in learning the single twist and slits. Tie off the yarn on the top dowel, the same dowel you started on, with a knot and slipknot, and leave a long end as before. This will give you an even number of threads. When you have warped all of the threads and tied off, remove the center cord (fig. 2–9).

Remove the masking tape and adjust the tension again if neccessary by pulling the threads around the dowels. If the tension is even but the threads are too loose or too tight, adjust by releasing or tightening the tension-release cords. As you sprang, you will get a feel for how tight the warp should be. This will depend on how tight or loose you want the twists to be and what type of yarn you are using.

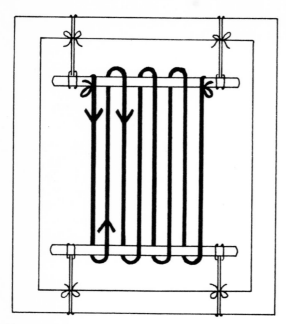

Fig. 2-9. Your completed warp should look like this but, of course, there will be many more warp threads, placed much closer together.

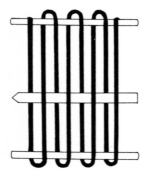

Fig. 2-10. When ready to begin spranging, place the shed stick between the bottom and top threads. The center cord can then be removed.

Put a long stick in the shed created by the lower dowel. The shed is the space between the threads in back of the dowel and the threads in front of the dowel. Since this stick holds the shed, it is called the shed stick. The first thread on the right side must be on top of the stick (fig. 2–10).

COLOR WARPING

Using more than one color or texture of yarn in a warp adds immeasurably to visual interest. Begin the warp with one color of yarn, tying on to the top dowel as usual. Warp as many threads as you wish. If you want an even number of threads of this color, cut and tie the yarn with a knot and slipknot to the top dowel. If you want an uneven number of threads, tie off on the bottom dowel. Tie the second color on the same dowel on which the first was tied off. The last color stripe on the right side of the warp must be tied off on the top dowel.

When the sprang is completed and before removing it from the frame, undo the knots and tie the end of one color of yarn to the end of the next. Use a square knot for strength and neatness. Clip the tied ends close. The two colors of yarn are not tied together while warping, as the knots would slip away from the dowels when the tension is adjusted.

The next chapter explains setting up and warping by the method of continuous warp, which enables you to sprang longer pieces. But for now, you're ready to sprang with the frame loom you have just set up. Go on to Chapter 4, which explains the first step in spranging.

Fig. 4-3. A warped frame made from stretchers. The shed stick is on top, and a single S twist is being spranged. The upper threads are held out of the way by the left hand while the right hand holds the pick-up stick and makes the twists.

USING YOUR EQUIPMENT

As you know, the long stick already inserted in the warp is called the shed stick, since it holds the shed in place. As you finish the twists, they will be transferred onto the other long stick. This stick is called the transfer stick. The two sticks will change roles each row, the shed stick becoming the transfer stick and the transfer stick becoming the shed stick. The purpose of these sticks will become more clear as you sprang the first two rows. The short stick is used to pick up threads and so is called the pick-up stick. You may use your fingers instead of the pick-up stick, if you like.

Always work from the bottom to the top of the frame. Since the frame rests between your lap and a table edge, this eliminates reaching. If you have ever done any weaving, you will also find this direction of work more logical. Work from the right side of the warp to the left.

Pick up a group of the upper threads from the top of the shed stick and hold these in your left hand as you work. This differentiates the upper threads from the lower threads, so you can't lose a thread.

TWO-ROW SEQUENCE

Have you ever tried to learn something new without first picking up the basics? No doubt you have found it quite difficult. If you didn't give up the whole project with frustration and disappointment, you probably started anew, learning the basic steps. This chapter will describe the most basic and most important steps in sprang. Remember these steps, and all the rest of your work will be easy and error free.

To emphasize them, the most important points will be *italicized*. First, *sprang is worked in a two-row sequence*. The first row is called the odd row. Rows 1, 3, 5, and so on will be odd rows. The first thread on the right side is up, on top of the shed stick.

There are two reasons why this is called an odd row. First, the number of the row itself is odd. Second and more important, the number of threads used in the first and last twists of the row is odd. Three threads are used in each of these twists whereas two are used in all of the other twists in the row.

The second row of the sequence is called the even row. Rows 2, 4, and 6 are even rows. The first two threads on the right are up. Again, there are two reasons why this row is designated as even. First, the number of the row is even. Second, the first and last twists use two threads, an even number, the same number used in all of the other twists in the row.

Odd row

1. The first row is an odd row. Using the short pick-up stick or your fingers, pick up the first two lower threads on the right edge. Pull these to the right and up (fig. 4–4). *Two lower threads are always picked up in the first twist in the odd row.*

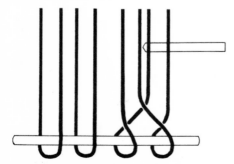

Fig. 4-4. Beginning the first single twist in the odd row.

2. Push down the first upper thread. The first twist is now completed and the thread that was pushed down is to the left of the two threads pulled up (fig. 4–5).

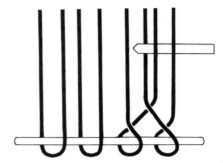

Fig. 4-5. Completing the first single twist in the odd row.

3. Pick up the next lower thread. Pick up only one thread, not two as when the row was started.

4. Push down the next upper thread. The second twist is completed. Again the thread that was pushed down is to the left of the one pulled up (fig. 4–6).

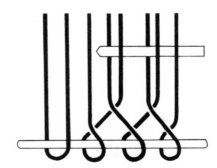

Fig. 4-6. Completing the second single twist in the odd row.

5. Pick up the next lower thread.

6. Continue making twists until the stick is full (fig. 4–7).

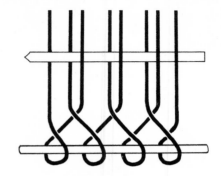

Fig. 4-7. Last twist in the odd row, completed.

Except for the first twist, only pick up one thread at a time. You will notice that *there is always one upper thread between the pair to be twisted* (fig. 4–8). If the upper thread is not between the pair to be twisted, you will know you have either dropped a thread or picked up an extra thread. Simply take out the twists back to the mistake and sprang them again.

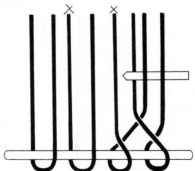

Fig. 4-8. The upper and lower thread for the next twist are marked by X's. One upper thread is always between them.

As you fill up the pick-up stick with twists, transfer the twists to the second long stick, the transfer stick. Do this by putting the short stick on edge and sliding in the transfer stick. Then, push the tip of the transfer stick *under* the untwisted warp, pointing up and away from you (fig. 4–9). This not only provides a clear view of the warp but makes for less chance of losing a thread.

Fig. 4-9. Transferring threads from pick-up stick to transfer stick. Always push the tip of the transfer stick under the untwisted warp, pointing away from you.

7. Continue across the row, making twists and transferring them to the transfer stick.

8. End the row by pulling up one lower thread and pushing down two upper threads. You started the row by picking up two threads and pushing down one. The row must be ended by picking up one thread and push-ing down two, so that the same number of threads will be up as are down. Another good indication that you have made a mistake in the row is not ending with two upper and one lower thread for the last twist in the odd row. Again, simply find the mistake, take out the twists back to that point, and sprang them over again.

9. Transfer the last twists onto the transfer stick.

All of the twists made are singles. Even the first and last twists, which used three threads each, are called singles. In the first twist on the right side, two threads were picked up and one pushed down. This is de-noted as 2/1, or two up and one down. In the last twist of the row, one thread was picked up and two pushed down. This is 1/2, or one up and two down.

Securing the twists

Before starting the second row, secure the twists in the first row.

1. Pull out the shed stick.
2. Turn the transfer stick on edge.
3. Pass a shed cord through the opening.
4. Push the cord to the bottom of the warp.
5. Turn the transfer stick on edge again.
6. Pass another cord through and push it to the top of the warp. Eventually these cords will be removed, but for now they serve to hold the twists in place.
7. Leave the transfer stick at the top of the warp. It is now the shed stick. The shed stick that you pulled out of the first row is now the transfer stick for the second row.

The top of the piece becomes a mirror image of the bottom. This effect can be dis-torted by pushing the cord more tightly to one end or the other. The last row will then not be in the exact center of the piece.

Even row

1. Row 2 is an even row. Pick up the first lower thread on the right side. *Only one lower thread is picked up in the first twist in even rows.*

2. Pull the thread to the right and up (fig. 4–10).

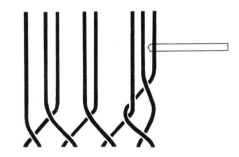

Fig. 4-10. Beginning the first twist in the even row that always follows the odd row. The shed cord holding the first row is not shown.

3. Push down the first upper thread. The thread pushed down is to the left of the one pulled up (fig. 4–11).

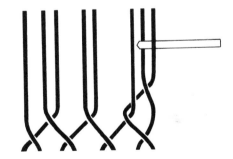

Fig. 4-11. Completing the first single twist in the even row.

4. Pick up the next lower thread.

5. Push down the next upper thread (fig. 4–12).

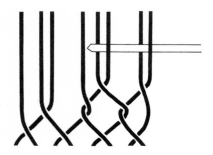

Fig. 4-12. Completing the second single twist in the even row.

6. Continue across the row, transferring the twists onto the transfer stick.

Notice again that there is always one upper thread between the pair to be twisted (fig. 4–13).

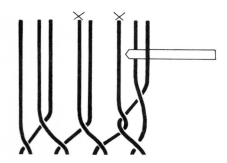

Fig. 4-13. One upper thread in the even row, too, is always between the pair to be twisted, marked by X's.

7. End the row by pulling up one lower thread and pushing down one upper thread (fig. 4–14).

If you do not end with one upper and one lower thread for the last twist in an even row, you know immediately you have made a mis-take in that row. Again, secure the twists with cords before going on to the next row.

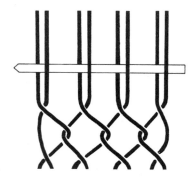

Fig. 4-14. Last twist in the even row, completed.

Row 3 is spranged just like Row 1, and Row 4 is spranged like Row 2. Do six or eight rows, always alternating odd and even. Keep three or four cords in the finished rows to hold them in place. This helps to keep the twists tight. Also, if you make a mistake or decide to change your design, as many rows of twists as necessary may be taken out. Remove the two cords last put in, and unravel the row of twists. Repeat this for the next row, and so on. Leave in at least two cords, one on top and one on bottom, that are closest to the dowels. Otherwise the whole piece will unravel. As you begin your work again, respranging the rows you have just removed, you will eventually remove these shed cords also, in the normal progression of the work. Pull out the other cords nearest the top and bottom dowels one at a time as the work progresses. The cord pulled out is used to hold the row just completed. Therefore, you only need three or four cords each for the top and bottom, since the cords are used again and again.

The tension will naturally tighten the closer you come to the center row. The tension can be released in two ways. Either take out the shed stick, release the tension release cords, or do both. The threads can be picked up from the shed cord. Using a crochet hook instead of the short pick-up stick or your fingers will also facilitate your work at this point.

You may want to use the rest of the warp to learn other twists or you may want to finish the warp using only singles. If you use singles, turn to page 27 for instructions on spranging the closing row. Chapter 14 describes other closings and how to take your work off the frame and block it. After you have taken it off the frame, play with the piece, twist it, turn it, shape it. What can you do with a sprang made from singles alone? Look at some of the photos—perhaps you might make a hat, a bag, or a placemat.

Fig. 4-15. Handbag, heavy and thin wool, Lisa Riden-our. Only singles are spranged, and a decorative fringe is added.

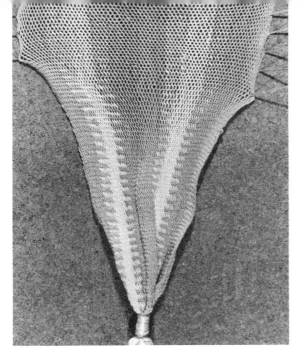

Fig. 4-16. Pakistani pajama string, fine cotton. The relaxed sprang at the bottom shows how it is worn. The pattern is produced by warping stripes of alternating colors between stripes of solid colors. (Collection of Jeannette Lund; photo by Kent Kammerer.)

Fig. 4-17. Detail of pajama string.

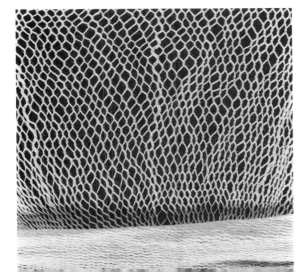

REVIEWING YOUR WORK

The four main steps to finishing and securing a row of twists will not be repeated, so review it now. Every row should be finished in the following manner:

1. As the row continues, transfer the twists to the transfer stick.
2. Pull out the shed stick.
3. Put in the shed cords and push them to the top and bottom.
4. Push the new shed stick to the top.

If you count the twists after you have done a row, you will find that the even row has one more twist than the odd row. This is because the first and last twists in the odd row use three threads each. An odd row with 40 threads makes 19 twists. An even row with the same number of threads makes 20 twists.

Notice that the twist on top is in the reverse direction from the one on the bottom. In the bottom half, the upper thread moves to the left, an S twist. In the top half, the upper thread moves to the right, a Z twist. As S twists are spranged at the bottom, Z twists are made at the top. Later, you will learn how to sprang Z twists, which will create S twists on the top half.

HELPFUL HINTS

Now that you have the basic sprang technique mastered, here are a few helpful hints to make the work easier.

Use a circular motion to bring the lower threads up. Put the stick or your finger under the lower thread and then slide your hand or stick towards you and over the upper thread. Push down the upper thread, then slide your hand or stick away from you and put your finger or stick under the next lower thread. Although it is referred to as picking up or pulling up, the lower thread is not really picked, but simply brought up in one continuous motion of bringing up and pushing down. This rhythmic up and down motion will come automatically with practice and will make the work smoother.

If you want a tight sprang, push down the previous rows before the cords have been pulled out. Use a fork, strong comb or your fingers. The tighter the twist, the greater will be the take-up, so you should allow for this by making a longer warp.

As you sprang more rows, the edges will begin to draw in. This makes it difficult to work the twists and to see the pattern. Use yarn or string as stretch cords, to tie the edges of the sprang to the sides of the frame, stretching the sprang back to its full width. The stretch cords should be tied a few rows below the row you are working on.

CLOSING ROW

If you have finished your warp, you need to sprang a closing row, which is the last row in the center and consists of a thread holding a row of twists. This thread secures all of the twists in the sprang and without it, the sprang would completely untwist. In Chapter 14, other closings such as looping are described.

The closing row is a continuation of the two-row sequence. If the previous row is odd, the closing row will be even. If the previous row is even, the closing row will be odd.

Thread a large needle with yarn two to three times the width of the sprang. The extra length of the closing thread may be used in finishing the piece, just as the long ends of the warp may be.

Closing row, even

Pick up the first lower thread on the right with the needle. Bring the needle over the first upper thread and pick up the next lower thread. Continue across the row, going over upper threads and picking up lower threads.

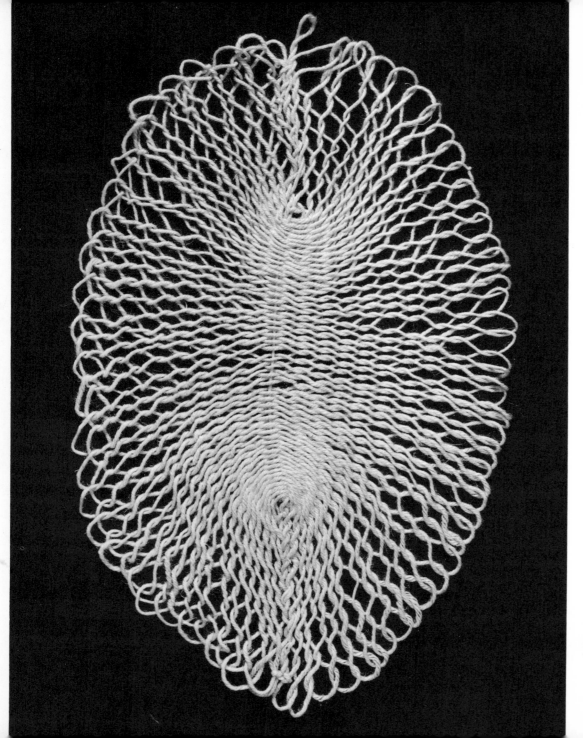

Closing row, odd

With the needle, pick up the first two lower threads on the right side. Bring the needle over the first upper thread and pick up the next lower thread. Continue across the row just as in an even closing row. End by picking up the last lower thread and going over the last two upper threads.

Close on an even row if possible. When an odd row is used to close, two threads are left up on the right side and two down on the left side.

Fig. 4-18. Mat, Thai jute, Mary Reddy. Spranged in singles only, with closing thread that pulls the center together. The long ends are used to join the sides into an oval shape.

5 Slits

The technique of making slits is the start of a fascinating world of sprang design. Using the single twist alone, you can create a beautiful and individual pattern with slits. This is done by interrupting the regular pattern, thereby making holes or openings in the fabric. It is not even necessary to learn a new twist to start creating designs with slits. They can be large or small, short or long; they can be arranged in any pattern throughout the piece.

Slits are formed by spranging in groups of singles within one row, each group beginning and ending like a row in itself. When the slit is started in the odd row, each group of singles starts 2/1 and ends 1/2; when started in the even row, each group of singles starts 2/1 and ends 1/2 except for the first and last twists of the row, which are spranged 1/1.

This gives each group its own edge. The space between groups is the slit. How many twists will be in each group is up to you, depending on your design. There is no set or specific number. A group of twists could consist of as few as two twists or a great number of twists, depending on how many you want.

Continue with the same warp unless you have used most of it. If you need a new warp, make it 40 threads wide (20 loops) and sprang two or four rows of singles, so as to place the threads in easy working order.

Fig. 5-1. Hanging, heavy linen, Hella Skowronski. The design is a symmetrical arrangement of slits within an area of singles.

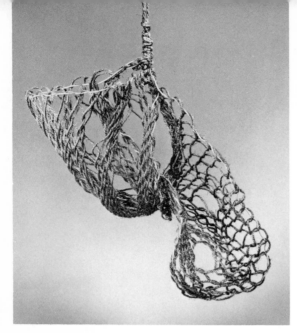

Fig. 5-2. Three-dimensional hanging, sisal, Hella Skowronski. The center is pulled together and the shape held by wire.

Fig. 5-3. Handbag, rattail and cloth, Lisa Ridenour. The closing is seen on the bottom; the cord that draws the bag closed is threaded through the loops that were at the top and bottom of the sprang.

MAKING SLITS

As always when spranging singles, it is very important to be aware of the two-row sequence. Not only do the first and last twists in the odd row use three threads, the two twists, one on either side of each opening, also use three threads. Slits can be started in the odd or even row but it is easier to start them in the odd row, as below.

In the practice example three groups will be spranged within each row, forming two slits. There is always one more group of singles than there are slits. If you made six groups in one row, you would have five slits. The following directions show how many twists to sprang within each group but later you will make up your own groupings, using as many twists within a group as you wish.

Odd row

In the example, the slits are begun in the odd row. The first odd row begins the two openings although they will not be immediately obvious.

GROUP ONE. Sprang the first twist 2/1. Sprang four more singles, for a total of five singles in group one. The last of these singles, the fifth twist, is spranged 1/2 (fig. 5–4). You have used 12 threads altogether.

GROUP TWO. Start the second group 2/1 (fig. 5–5). Sprang six more singles, making a total of seven singles spranged. The seventh twist is spranged 1/2. You have used 16 threads in this group.

GROUP THREE. Start 2/1. Sprang four more singles, for a total of five singles in group three. The fifth twist is 1/2, and 12 threads have been used.

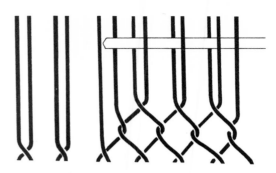

Fig. 5-4. Ending the first group of twists before a slit in an odd row.

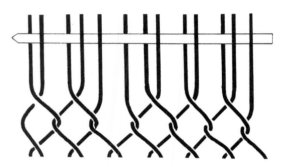

Fig. 5-5. Beginning the second group of twists, after the slit, in an odd row. Two twists of the second group are shown.

In the last chapter, each odd row began 2/1 and ended 1/2. When making slits, each group within an odd row begins 2/1 and ends 1/2.

Even row

Sprang singles across the full row. All of the twists, including the first and last, are spranged 1/1 (fig. 5-6).

Subsequent rows

The next odd row is spranged in the same way as the first row, with the same number

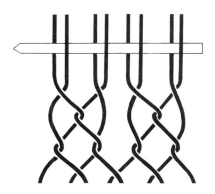

Fig. 5-6. Two groups of twists, before and after the slit, in an even row. The row is spranged as an ordinary even row, and the slits formed in the odd row begin to appear.

of twists and threads. The slits that have formed between the groups should now be apparent.

The next even row is spranged just like the previous even row. Notice that each group has one more twist in the even row than in the odd row. For example, the first group has five twists in the odd row and six twists in the even row.

Beginning slits in even row

After completing the example, try starting slits in the even row. The first group of singles in the even row begins 1/1 and ends 1/2. The last group of singles begins 2/1 and ends 1/1. All groups between begin 2/1 and end 1/2.

CLOSING SLITS

There are three ways to close the openings. Until you are more experienced, however, use only one method to close both slits; later you can effectively combine the different methods.

After you have used one method to close the slits, you will have to make new slits to try the other methods. Simply repeat the above pattern of odd and even rows to make new slits.

In the following examples, the slits are closed in the odd row. This is necessary because the slits were started in an odd row. If they had been started in an even row, they would have to be closed in an even row.

Method 1—closing all slits

Begin the row 2/1. Sprang 1/1 across the whole row, spranging the last twist 1/2.

Method 2—leaving one slit open

To leave the first slit open, begin the row 2/1 and sprang singles to the first slit (five twists). End the group by spranging the fifth twist 1/2.

To close the second slit, start the group 2/1. Sprang singles to the second slit but do not sprang 1/2 on the seventh twist. Instead, continue over the second slit, closing it by spranging 1/1 to the end of the row. To get from the first slit to the end of the row, you sprang 13 singles. End the group 1/2 on the thirteenth twist. With a greater number of slits in your work, you can alternate opening and closing in your own pattern.

Method 3—diagonal slits

Diagonal slits are formed when a slit is closed and a new one is started on the left or right side of it.

GROUP 1. Start the row 2/1 and sprang six more singles. Make seven singles in all (16 threads). End this group 1/2 on the seventh twist. A new slit will form to the left of the previous one (fig. 5–7).

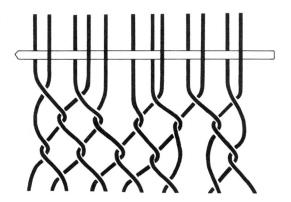

Fig. 5-7. Forming a diagonal slit to the left of the one in the previous row.

GROUP 2. Start the group 2/1. Sprang two more singles, making a total of three singles (eight threads) in this group. The third twist is spranged 1/2. A new slit will be formed to the right of the previous one (fig. 5–8).

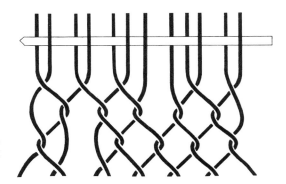

Fig. 5-8. Forming a diagonal slit to the right.

GROUP 3. Start the group 2/1. Sprang six more singles, so that seven singles are spranged. End the row 1/2.

Close the new slits when they are as many rows high as you want, and use any of the closings described. Perhaps you will want to make more diagonal slits to the right or left of the ones you have just made. Here are a few simple rules to follow so that you can make diagonal slits no matter how many twists you have in each group.

New slit to the left of the old one.

1. Sprang to the slit to be closed, leaving one thread up to the right of the slit.

2. Then, sprang 1/1, bringing up the lower thread on the left of the slit and pushing down the upper thread to the right of the slit. This closes the previous slit.

3. End the group by spranging 1/2.

4. Begin the next group 2/1.

New slit to the right of the old one.

1. Sprang singles to the slit to be closed but leave four upper threads and three lower threads untwisted on the right of the slit.

2. Using the untwisted threads, sprang 1/2. This leaves two upper threads and two lower threads untwisted to the right of the slit.

3. Again using the untwisted threads, sprang 2/1, beginning the next group. The next 1/1 closes the previous slit.

DESIGNING IN SPRANG

Sometimes you will sprang "off the top of your head," creating the pattern as you work. Other times, you will want to work the pattern out carefully in advance. If you want to plan your pattern, remember one rule: A group of twists must always consist of an even number of threads. This is necessary because in any group of twists there must be the same number of upper and lower threads. For example, if your sprang contains 40 threads, a slit can be placed exactly in the center, with 20 threads (an even number) on either side. A warp of 42 threads will not allow for a slit precisely in the center.

The number, size, and placement of the slits add interest to a piece. Numerous small slits can be spranged—in fact, you can sprang 1/2 and 2/1 continuously across the whole row. Small slits can be contrasted with large ones, or you can make a simple design with a few large, well-balanced slits. Shells and beads can be attached to the top of the openings, using needle and yarn or thread (fig. 5–9). The openings can be enhanced by backing a hanging, pillow, or purse with fabric of a similar or contrasting color. You might crochet or embroider around some or all of the openings to add more emphasis to the structural quality (fig. 5–10), to provide extra texture (fig. 5–11), or to bring in another color. Slits alone offer countless possibilities.

Fig. 5-9. Hanging, mohair, Lyn Lambert. A simple structure of singles is made interesting by its framing and by the shell in one of the openings.

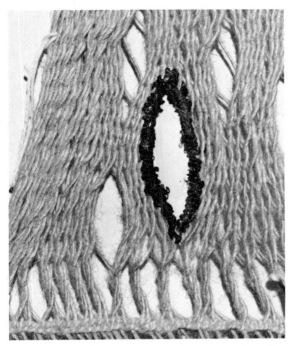

Fig. 5-10. Stitchery used around the rim of a slit.

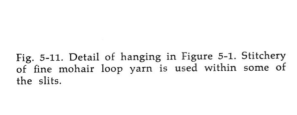

Fig. 5-11. Detail of hanging in Figure 5-1. Stitchery of fine mohair loop yarn is used within some of the slits.

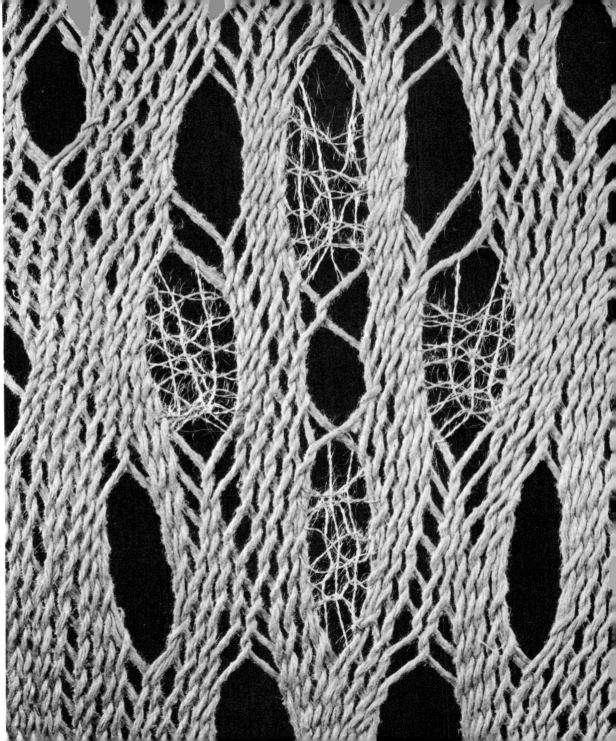

6 Doubles

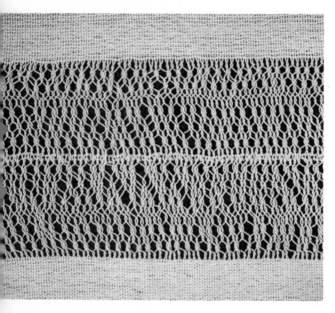

Fig. 6-1. Rows of doubles and singles, with a looped closing at the back that hardly shows. This is a detail of sprang and weaving combined, Figure 15-7.

By now you are beginning to know sprang, from yarn to warp to finished piece, and you have felt the excitement of seeing the results of your new craft. If, along the way, you feel that your sprang is less than you hoped, keep on trying! Even the best painter has to learn how to apply the paint before he can use it with imagination. Learn the techniques of sprang, and you soon will find that it will do what you wish.

In the meantime, there is much to be enjoyed. Like all textile crafts, spranging is a sensory experience. See the beauty of solid or blended areas of color in the growing structure of your work. Learn to appreciate the feeling of the different sizes and textures of your yarns.

Of course, the more techniques you learn, the more you will be able to command sprang to express what you want. The double twist adds many design possibilities to your repertoire. To get you started, four different double-twist patterns are described below.

The single twist was made by picking up one thread and pushing down another. The double is made in the same way, except that two threads are picked up at one time and two threads are pushed down. Because there are four threads in each twist, the warp should be in multiples of four. Doubles will be denoted as *d,* or 2/2, or two up, two down.

Unlike singles, you do not have to worry about the odd and even rows when spranging only doubles across a row. The first and last twists always involve an even number of threads, two or four. In essence, all rows are even. In a later chapter, doubles and singles will be combined in the same row, and odd and even will become an important factor again, as it always is when using singles.

PLAIN DOUBLES

In the first row, all of the twists, even the first and last, are exactly the same, using four threads each. For this reason, the row is called plain doubles. Sprang the first row in the following manner.

1. Pick up the first two lower threads on the right. Pull these to the right and up (fig. 6–2).

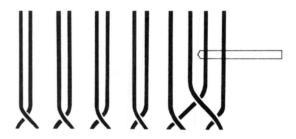

Fig. 6-2. Beginning the double twist. There is no odd or even row when spranging doubles.

2. Push down the first two upper threads. The first twist has been completed. Notice that the threads you pushed down are now to the left of the ones you pulled up (fig. 6–3).

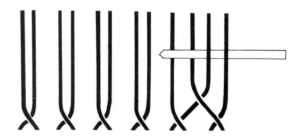

Fig. 6-3. Completing the first double twist.

3. Pick up the next two lower threads. Pull them to the right and up.

4. Push down the next two upper threads (fig. 6–4). Now that the second twist is completed, the threads pushed down are again to the left of those pulled up.

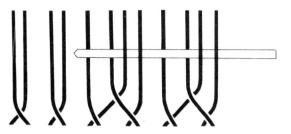

Fig. 6-4. Completing the second double twist.

5. Continue in this manner across the whole row.

Of course, it is necessary to know how to sprang plain doubles if you want to sprang a pattern of doubles. However, it is handy for another reason. If you ever get lost in a sprang piece or make a mistake too far back to correct, simply sprang a row of plain doubles and your threads will be back in working order. This technique can be used no matter which twist you happen to be spranging at the time.

PATTERNS

There are four ways to continue after spranging the first row of plain doubles, each of which creates a special pattern effect. Singles are also used but not in the same row as the doubles. Each pattern begins with a row of plain doubles, although it is not absolutely necessary to start this way. But it is easier when beginning, as it sets up the pattern.

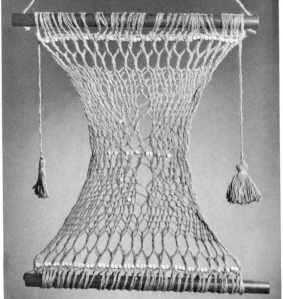

Fig. 6-5. Hanging, linen and wooden beads, Hella Skowronski. Pattern 1—ropes—is used for the top and bottom.

Pattern 1—ropes

1. Sprang the first row in plain doubles.

2. To sprang the second row, pick up and twist the same four threads as in the first row (fig. 6–6). This gives a rope effect if done for a number of rows.

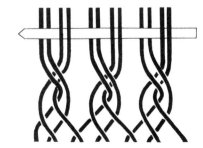

Fig. 6-6. Pattern 1—ropes. The ropes can be lengthened by using this double-twist pattern in succeeding rows.

3. If you wish, lengthen the rope effect by continuing to twist the same four threads in succeeding rows.

4. An interesting effect can be achieved at this point by spranging the first twist of the next row 4/2. Then, sprang 2/2 across the row, ending 2/4. All of the lower threads of one double are twisted with all of the upper threads of the previous double. You can now begin a new set of ropes.

5. Another interesting effect is possible using even singles. Sprang an even row of singles between each row of doubles. The ropes are flatter and take on a more textured appearance.

6. Finally, you may wish to stop the rope pattern. The easiest way to do this is to sprang an odd row of singles, as in Pattern 2 —diamonds. However, the ropes can also be split by doubles, as in Pattern 4—floating threads.

Pattern 2—diamonds

This pattern splits the doubles with an odd row of singles. Diamonds form across each row, each diamond in the row of singles being divided by a vertical line consisting of one single twist.

1. Sprang plain doubles in the first row.

2. The second row is an odd row of singles. Begin the row 2/1. Then, pick up the first lower thread of the second double. Push down the last upper thread of the first double. Next, pick up the last lower thread of the second double and push down the first upper thread of the second double. There is always either one upper or lower thread remaining from the double which has been split. This is because the first single twist used three threads. Continue across with singles, forming the last twist 1/2 (fig. 6–7).

35

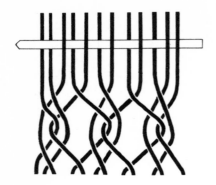

Fig. 6-7. Pattern 2—diamonds. The second row of the pattern is spranged as odd singles.

3. Row 3 is spranged just like Row 1 (fig. 6–8) and Row 4 like Row 2.

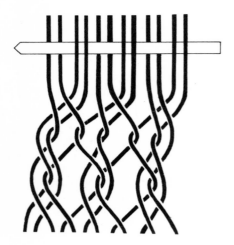

Fig. 6-8. Pattern 2—diamonds. The third row is spranged as plain doubles.

Pattern 3—large diamonds

Pattern 3 splits the doubles by a row of even singles. The design formed is exceptionally striking because of its bold openwork effect.

1. Sprang the first row in plain doubles.
2. In the second row, sprang an even row of singles. Begin this row 1/1. The first upper thread and the first lower thread of the first double make one single twist. The last upper thread and last lower thread of the first double make the second single (fig. 6–9). Continue across the row.

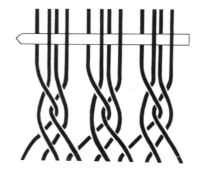

Fig. 6-9. Pattern 3—large diamonds. The second row is spranged in even singles.

3. Sprang Row 3 in doubles, except for the first twist, which is spranged 1/1. Pick up the next two lower threads and push down the next two upper threads. Continue across the row in this manner. The last twist is spranged 1/1 (fig. 6–10).

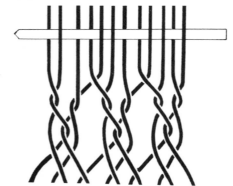

Fig. 6-10. Pattern 3—large diamonds; completing the third row.

4. For Row 4, return to an even row of singles, beginning the row 1/1.
5. Repeat the whole pattern, if you wish.

Fig. 6-11. Vest, wool, Aves Pickering. A complex structure was created from rows of doubles and singles. For details of construction of shaped vests see Figures 14-25, 14-26, and 14-27.

Fig. 6-12. Vest, tightly twisted wool, Aves Pickering. Spranged in two pieces in rows of doubles and singles, it was later joined at the sides. The rope at the waistline is threaded through one of the closings.

Pattern 4—floating threads

Pattern 4 splits the doubles in one row by doubles in the next. Two threads from each of the doubles of the first row run vertically through all of the succeeding rows. An interesting effect can be achieved by warping these two threads in a contrasting or coordinating color in order to emphasize them. Try the pattern first, though, in one color. Warping the floating threads as separate colors entails a good deal of tying on and off.

1. As before, sprang the first row in plain doubles.

2. Begin the second row 1/1. This will split the first double. Continue across with 2/2. This is done by picking up the last lower thread from the first double and the first lower thread from the next double, and pushing down the last upper thread from the first double and the first upper thread from the next double. This splits all doubles. Two threads will be left at the end of the row, which are spranged 1/1 (fig. 6–13).

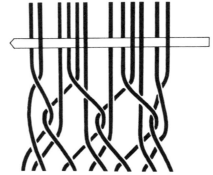

Fig. 6-13. Pattern 4—floating threads; completing the second row.

3. Repeat the sequence of Rows 1 and 2.

Variations

Repeat or mix these patterns as you wish, and you can achieve unlimited variety. Vary the order of the patterns. Perhaps in one piece you will sprang Pattern 2, then Pattern 3, then Pattern 1, ending with Pattern 4. Another time you might sprang just Patterns 1 and 4, repeating them over and over.

Make some segments longer than the others by repeating the pattern. For instance, if you want to emphasize the rope effect, sprang Pattern 1 for a number of rows. If you want to stress the design using even singles, repeat Pattern 3—large diamonds—once or twice. No doubt you can make your own patterns using variations on those described.

Fig. 6-14. Tunic, wool and velvet, Lisa Ridenour. In a clever use of sprang, the warp is turned horizontally. Unspranged warp in center was partially closed and partially wrapped with yarn. The top of the sprang is at one side of the tunic, stitched to the backing, and the bottom is at the other side. The back was made separately.

7 Trebles

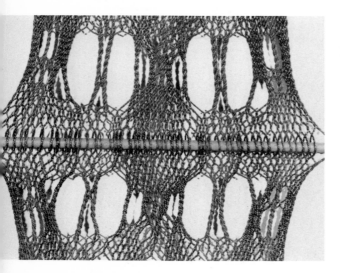

Fig. 7-1. Detail of hanging using Pattern 1—ropes. A dowel makes an effective closing. The complete hanging by Hella Skowronski is shown in color on page 11.

The treble is a fascinating twist, as simple to make as a single or double but even more complicated in structure. You probably have already guessed that three lower threads are picked up and three upper threads are pushed down, each twist involving six threads. Because of the number of threads used in each twist, the treble can be split in even more ways than the double, making it the most versatile twist. The treble is referred to as *t*, or 3/3.

Just as when spranging doubles across a full row, the terms odd and even are not important when spranging trebles across a full row. In the nine basic patterns, the first and last twists in the treble row use an even number of threads, two, four, or six. Since all of the treble rows are even, there is no need for differentiation. Some variations on the basic patterns are described below, in which the first and last twists may use an uneven number of threads.

PLAIN TREBLES

For trebles, the warp should be in multiples of six, as there are six threads in each twist. However, some of the patterns use doubles in the second row. The warp for doubles must be in multiples of four. To accommodate both twists, make your warp in multiples of twelve, as both six and four threads can be evenly divided into twelve.

In the first row, all of the trebles, even the first and last twists, use six threads each, three upper threads and three lower threads. Here is how to sprang plain trebles.

1. Pick up the first three lower threads. Pull to the right and up.
2. Push down the first three upper threads.
3. Pick up the next three lower threads.
4. Push down the next three upper threads.
5. Continue in this manner to the end of the row.

PATTERNS

Although there are many variations, nine patterns are described below, in which trebles are spranged across a full row. Singles and dou-

bles are also used but not in the same row as the trebles. Chapter 9 will describe how to combine trebles and singles in the same row.

The row that follows the plain trebles splits the treble twists. The treble can be split by singles, doubles, or another row of trebles. Each of the nine patterns begins with a row of plain trebles. As with doubles, it is not necessary to begin this way, but it is easier when learning, as it sets up the pattern.

Pattern 1—ropes

Fig. 7-2. Another detail of the same hanging, showing a variation on the rope pattern. Upper threads of each rope are twisted with the lower threads of the adjacent rope and then twisted together again, creating the diamond-shaped openings.

1. Sprang the first row in plain trebles.
2. To sprang the second row, twist the same six threads as you twisted in Row 1 (fig. 7–3). Because there are more threads in each twist, the rope effect is more pronounced than in doubles.

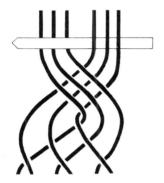

Fig. 7-3. Pattern 1–ropes. As with doubles, the rope can be made as long as desired by continuing Pattern 1 in succeeding rows.

3. Lengthen the rope effect by continuing to twist the same six threads in succeeding rows.
4. To begin a new set of ropes, splitting the first set, sprang the first twist 6/3. Continue across the row with 3/3. All of the lower threads of one treble are twisted with all of the upper threads of the previous treble. The last twist is 3/6.
5. The ropes will take on a more textured appearance if you sprang an even row of singles between each row of trebles.
6. Finally, to stop the ropes and start a new pattern, sprang an odd row of singles, a row of doubles, or one of trebles. The following patterns describe these variations.

Pattern 2—diamonds

This pattern splits the trebles with an odd row of singles, forming a diamond design across each row. Each diamond in the single rows is divided by a strong vertical line consisting of two adjacent single twists.
1. Sprang the first row in plain trebles.
2. In the second row, sprang an odd row of singles, starting 2/1 and ending 1/2. Except for the first and last trebles of the row, the first lower thread of a treble always twists with the third upper thread of the last treble. The second lower thread twists with the first upper thread of the same treble. The third lower thread twists with the second upper thread of the same treble (fig. 7–4).
3. Lengthen the pattern by repeating Rows 1 and 2.

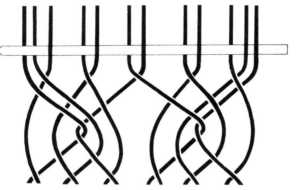

Fig. 7-4. Pattern 2—diamonds. The second row is spranged in odd singles.

Pattern 3—large diamonds

Pattern 3 forms a very open design of large diamonds. It is created by spranging an even row of singles between each row of trebles.
1. Sprang the first row in plain trebles.
2. In the second row, sprang even singles. As always when spranging even singles, the row begins and ends 1/1. The first upper and first lower threads of each treble twist over each other. The second upper and lower threads of each treble make another single twist. The third upper and lower threads of each treble also form a single.
3. Sprang Row 3 in trebles, but start the row 2/2 and end the row 1/1.
4. As in Row 2, sprang an even row of singles.
5. Continue the pattern by repeating Rows 1–4.
6. A slight variation in the appearance of this pattern can be made by spranging Row 3 in trebles, but beginning 1/1 and ending 2/2. All of the other rows in this variation are spranged in exactly the same way as above.

Pattern 4—arches

Here, the trebles are split by doubles. The structure of this pattern is truly beautiful. The first row of doubles forms openings between the second and third trebles of the previous row, between the fourth and fifth trebles of the previous row, and so on. The intricate design of interlacing threads, vertical threads, and arches gives an almost Gothic appearance.
1. Sprang the first row in plain trebles.
2. Sprang the second row in doubles, starting 2/2 and ending 2/2.
3. Sprang Row 3 in doubles, starting 1/1 and ending 1/1. This row closes the openings made in Row 2.
4. Repeat Rows 1–3 to continue the pattern. When Row 4 is spranged in plain trebles, like Row 1, openings become obvious between the first and second trebles, between the third and fourth trebles, and so on.

Pattern 5—variation on arches

Like Pattern 4, the trebles are split by doubles. Rows 2 and 3 are simply spranged in the reverse order from that of Pattern 4. The first row of doubles forms openings between the first and second trebles of the previous row, between the third and fourth trebles of the previous row, and so on.

1. Sprang Row 1 in plain trebles.
2. Sprang Row 2 in doubles. The first twist is spranged 1/1. This splits the first treble. Finish the row, spranging 2/2. The last twist is spranged 1/1.
3. Sprang Row 3 in doubles also, beginning 2/2 and ending 2/2 (fig. 7–5). This row closes the openings made in Row 2.

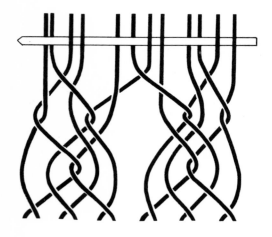

Fig. 7-5. Pattern 5—variation on arches. The second and third row of this treble pattern are spranged in doubles.

4. Continue the pattern by repeating Rows 1–3. When Row 4 is spranged in plain trebles, openings appear between the second and third trebles, between the fourth and fifth trebles, and so on.

Pattern 6—floating threads

This pattern splits the trebles in one row by trebles in the next. Three threads from each of the trebles of Row 1 float vertically through all of the succeeding rows. It is interesting to warp these three threads in a different color for emphasis.

1. Sprang the first row in plain trebles.
2. Sprang the first twist of the second row 2/2. Sprang the remainder of the row in 3/3, except for the last twist, which is 1/1. One upper and one lower thread are always left from the treble which has been split (fig. 7–6).

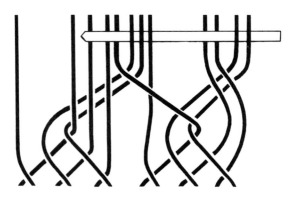

Fig. 7-6. Pattern 6—floating threads. The first twist of the second row is a double.

3. Lengthen the pattern by repeating Rows 1 and 2.

Pattern 7—variation on floating threads

Pattern 7 also splits one row of trebles by another row of trebles. Again, threads from the first row of trebles float vertically through all succeeding rows.

1. Sprang the first row in plain trebles.
2. Sprang the first twist in the second row 1/1. Continue across with 3/3. The last twist is spranged 2/2 (fig. 7–7). Two upper and two lower threads are always left from the treble which has been split.

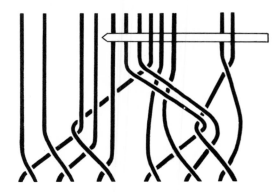

Fig. 7-7. Pattern 7—variation on floating threads. The first twist in the second row is a single.

3. Continue the pattern by repeating Rows 1 and 2.

Pattern 8—diagonal ridges in back

The trebles are again split by trebles. The front of the sprang has a delicate appearance, with some of the threads floating vertically for two rows and others crossing diagonally. The back of the piece is less delicate, as strong diagonal ridges form.

1. Sprang the first row in plain trebles.
2. Sprang trebles in the second row, beginning 2/2 and ending 1/1.
3. Sprang trebles in Row 3, beginning 1/1 and ending 2/2 (fig. 7–8).

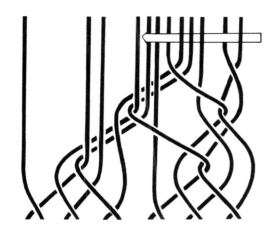

Fig. 7-8. Pattern 8—diagonal ridges in back. The third row is in trebles, beginning with a single and ending with a double.

4. Repeat rows 1–3 to lengthen the pattern.

Pattern 9—diagonal ridges in front

Pattern 9 is like Pattern 8 except that Rows 2 and 3 are spranged in reverse. Like Pattern 8, some of the threads float vertically for two rows and others form a cross-hatched pattern. The difference is that the diagonal ridges appear on the front, rather than the back, of the piece.

1. Sprang plain trebles in the first row.

2. In the second row, sprang the first twist 1/1. Continue across the row with 3/3, splitting all trebles. The last twist is spranged 2/2.

3. Sprang Row 3 in trebles, making the first twist 2/2. Continue across the row with 3/3, and sprang the last twist 1/1.

4. Lengthen the pattern by repeating Rows 1–3.

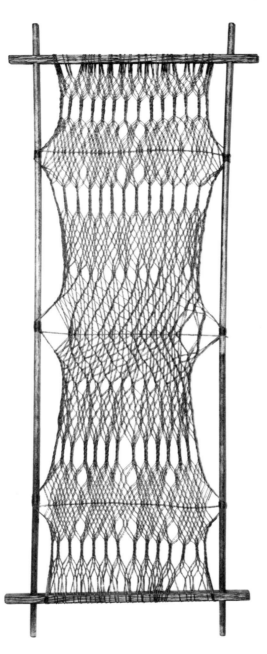

Fig. 7-9. Hanging, fine perle cotton, Lyn Lambert. The center sections are spranged in Pattern 9—diagonal ridges in front. The ropes separating these sections are in Pattern 1.

VARIATIONS

These nine patterns give the basic ways to split the twists in the row of trebles. However, numerous variations can be played on these main themes. Try some of the following.

Variation 1

Row 1 (trebles)	begin 3/3	end 3/3
2 (trebles)	2/1	1/2
3 (trebles)	1/1	2/2

Variation 2

Row 1 (trebles)	begin 3/3	end 3/3
2 (trebles)	1/1	2/2
3 (trebles)	2/1	1/2

Variation 3

Row 1 (trebles)	begin 3/3	end 3/3
2 (trebles)	3/1	3/5
3 (trebles)	1/1	2/2

Variation 4

Row 1 (trebles)	begin 3/3	end 3/3
2 (trebles)	1/1	2/2
3 (trebles)	3/1	3/5

Variation 5

Row 1 (trebles)	begin 3/3	end 3/3
2 (trebles)	1/1	2/2
3 (trebles)	3/2	3/4

Variation 6

Row 1 (trebles)	begin 3/3	end 3/3
2 (doubles)	2/1	1/2

Variation 7

Row 1 (trebles)	begin 3/3	end 3/3
2 (doubles)	2/1	1/2
3 (doubles)	1/1	1/1

41

8 Doubles and Singles

Fig. 8-1. Poncho, wool, Hella Skowronski. Spranged in one piece of five sections, each section was started with S twists. The neck opening is one large slit with a closing on both sides. The bottom, and therefore the top, was left unspranged to provide long loops for the fringe.

You have already learned how to make intricate and beautiful designs by spranging a full row of one kind of twist followed by a full row of the same or another kind of twist. But the combinations in sprang do not end there; to achieve an even more intricate structure, two or more types of twist are combined in the same row, and each offsets and compliments the other.

Any number of patterns can be achieved by combining the single and double twist, some rather closed and subtle, others very open and lacy. From row to row the pattern can move diagonally, to give sideways direction to the design, or it can move vertically and horizontally, in which case the right angles create strong geometric designs. Small areas of one

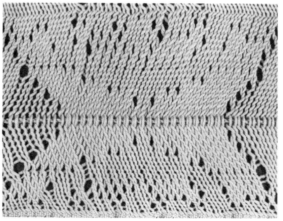

Fig. 8-2. Detail of poncho. Doubles and singles are spranged together in every row as in Method 4—floating threads.

type of twist may be spranged within a surrounding area of another twist, or a large, dominant design of one twist may be bordered by another twist. The diamond design described in Method 4 is an example of this.

WORK PROCEDURES

The five methods described are all set up in much the same way. A warp of 60 threads is used. As you know, whenever spranging doubles, the warp should be in a multiple of four, as there are four threads in each twist.

In each of the examples, one group of doubles is spranged with one group of singles to the right and one group of singles to the left. It is usually preferable to sprang singles on the edges, as they draw in less than doubles. Once you have mastered the different methods and are forming your own designs, you may certainly sprang more than one group of doubles within a row.

The terms odd and even were not used in learning how to sprang doubles across a full row. When singles are combined in the same row with doubles, however, it is again important to be aware of the two-row sequence, as it always is when singles are used.

Directions will be given in a very abbreviated fashion. The number in parenthesis refers to the number of threads used in a group. Let's look at an example:

Row 2 (even)—8 *s* (16), 5 *d* (20), 12 *s* (24) This means that in Row 2, an even row, eight singles are spranged on the *right* side, using 16 threads. Then five doubles are spranged in the same row, using 20 threads. The last group on the *left* of the piece consists of 12 singles, using 24 threads. In a warp of 60 threads, the numbers in parenthesis always add up to 60.

All of the patterns in this chapter begin with two rows of singles, as this puts the warp threads into easy working order. This does not mean that you have to use a new warp for every example—full designs are not given except in Method 4. Instead, the first few rows, just enough so you can continue on by yourself, are given in each example in the five methods.

METHOD 1—DIAMONDS

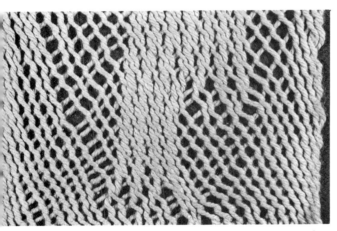

Fig. 8-3. Method 1—diamonds. The pattern area has been moved vertically and increased to the right.

Odd row:
  singles only, begin 2/1 and end 1/2
Even row:
  right side: singles, begin and end 1/1
  center: doubles
  left side: singles, begin and end 1/1
This is a very versatile method. The doubles can move either vertically or diagonally, and in each case the appearance is quite different.

Vertical stripes

When the pattern moves vertically, with the same number of singles and doubles in each even row, structural stripes of singles and doubles are formed. To emphasize these stripes you might warp the area of doubles in a different color. You would then have both structural and color stripes. The singles spranged in the odd row are very apparent within the doubles area, forming straight vertical lines running the length of the stripe.

The width of the stripes will remain the same as long as the same number of doubles and singles are spranged in each even row. However, increasing or decreasing the number of doubles will also increase or decrease the width of the stripe. Using this method, you can develop simple or complex patterns of squares and rectangles.

Since all the examples begin with two rows of singles, and since the third row in this method is odd, and all odd rows are spranged in singles only, this example begins with three rows of singles: an odd, an even, and an odd.
  Rows 1, 2, and 3—s only
  Row 4 (even)—12 s (24), 4 d (16), 10 s (20)
  Row 5 (odd)—s only
  Row 6 (even)—12 s (24), 4 d (16), 10 s (20)
  Row 7 (odd)—s only
So far, the pattern moves straight up. To make the stripes longer, simply repeat Rows 4–7 as often as you wish.

Increasing or decreasing width of vertical stripe

To increase the width of the stripe of doubles and continue the pattern vertically, decrease one or both groups of singles by an *even* number of single twists. The same number of threads, not twists, must be taken from a group of singles as are added to the doubles. For every two single twists (four threads) subtracted, one double twist (four threads)

can be added. For example, you may want to make the stripe of doubles wider by adding two doubles (eight threads) to the left of the stripe. The group of singles on the left must then be decreased by four twists (eight threads).

In the following example (see fig. 8–3), the group of singles on the right is decreased by six twists (12 threads) because three doubles (12 threads) are added to the right.
  Row 8 (even)—6 s (12), 7 d (28), 10 s (20)
  Row 9 (odd)—s only
Repeat Rows 8 and 9 if you wish to lengthen this stripe of doubles.

To make the stripe of doubles narrower and continue the pattern vertically, increase one or both groups of singles by an even number of twists. For every double (four threads) taken from the doubles area, two singles (four threads) must be added to one or both groups of singles. If you want to decrease the group of doubles by one double on each side, two singles should be added to the groups of singles on both the right and left.

In the following example (fig. 8–4), four doubles (16 threads) are taken from the left of the stripe of doubles (in Rows 8 and 9) and eight singles (16 threads) are added to the singles on the left.

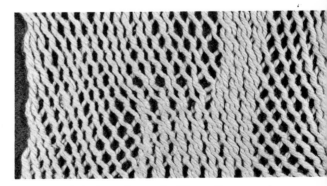

Fig. 8-4. Method 1—diamonds. The pattern area has been moved vertically while decreasing the left side.

43

Row 10 (even)—6 s (12), 3 d (12), 18 s (36)
Row 11 (odd)—s only

Repeat Rows 10 and 11 to lengthen this stripe.

Moving doubles diagonally

When the doubles move diagonally, a completely different appearance is given to the stripe of doubles. The singles in the odd row no longer show up as vertical lines. Instead, a pattern is formed of small diamond shapes inside of larger hexagonal shapes.

To move the doubles diagonally, simply increase one group of singles by an *odd* number of twists and decrease the other group by the same odd number of twists. To move the pattern to the left, using the same number of doubles in each row, the singles on the left should be decreased while the singles on the right are increased by the same number of twists, whether it be one, three, five or a greater odd number. The larger the number by which you decrease one group of singles and increase the other, the more gradual (closer to horizontal) is the diagonal movement.

In the following example (figs. 8–5 and 8–6), the doubles move diagonally to the right. In each even row, the singles on the right are decreased by three twists and the singles on the left are increased by three twists.

Rows 1, 2 and 3—s only
Row 4 (even)—15 s (30), 5 d (20), 5 s (10)
Row 5 (odd)—s only
Row 6 (even)—12 s (24), 5 d (20), 8 s (16)
Row 7 (odd)—s only
Row 8 (even)—9 s (18), 5 d (20), 11 s (22)

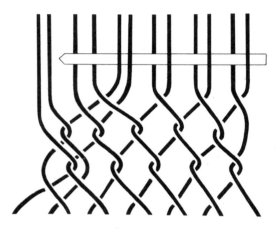

Fig. 8-5. Method 1—diamonds; moving the double to the right by one single twist in each even row.

Fig. 8-6. Method 1—diamonds. The pattern area has been moved diagonally.

Moving doubles diagonally and changing width

You can also move the doubles diagonally and increase or decrease the width of the doubles area at the same time. Increases and decreases are made by an odd number of single twists, as using an even number would create right angle patterns. It is not difficult to determine the number of twists by which one of the groups of singles should be changed. First, decide how many doubles you want to add to the stripe of doubles. As previously mentioned, for every double (four threads) added, two single twists (four threads) are taken from one of the groups of singles. If you want to add one double on the left, the singles on the left must be decreased by two twists.

Next determine if you want to move the pattern by one, three, five, or more single twists. If you decide to move the pattern to the left by three twists, three singles will have to be subtracted from the left-hand singles and three added to the right-hand singles. Then you will have to combine the two operations, adding doubles and moving the pattern to the left or right, to come up with the correct number of twists in each stripe.

Here is an example. One double is added on the right and the pattern is moved to the right by ten threads. You might think of this as two sets of additions and subtractions.

left side	middle	right side
same number of threads	+ 4 threads	− 4 threads (This adds one double to right.)
+ 10 threads	same number of threads	− 10 threads (This moves pattern to right by ten threads.)
+ 10 threads	+ 4 threads	− 14 threads (This combines the two changes.)

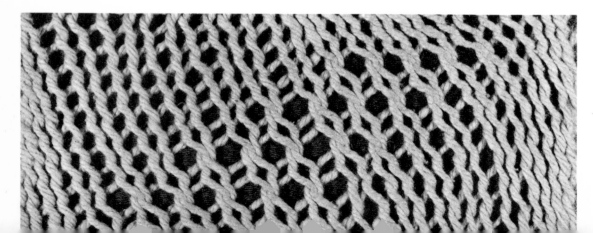

Ten threads (five singles) are added on the left and 14 threads (seven singles) are subtracted from the right. This will automatically add one double and move the pattern to the right by ten threads.

A good way of checking your pattern, whether you do the figuring by common sense in your head or write it out, is to realize that however many twists you move will be added to one side while the other side shows the double effect of moving and changing the number of doubles.

METHOD 2—LARGE DIAMONDS

Fig. 8-7. Method 2—large diamonds. The pattern moves diagonally left or right.

Odd rows:

right side:	singles, begin 2/1 and end 1/2
center:	doubles
left side:	singles, begin 2/1 and end 1/2

Even row:

singles only, begin and end 1/1

Method 2 forms a lovely, open design, the area of doubles sparkling in rows of diamonds. Openings form between the groups of doubles and singles. This is the case whenever the first group of singles ends 1/2 and the second group of singles begins 2/1.

The pattern moves diagonally left or right, the doubles moving over by an odd number of single twists in every odd row. To move the pattern to the right by one single twist, decrease the singles on the right by one twist (two threads) and increase the singles on the left by one twist (two threads). To move the pattern to the left by one single twist, as in the example below (see fig. 8–7), do just the opposite, decreasing the left-hand singles by two threads and increasing the right-hand singles by two threads (fig. 8–8).

Rows 1 and 2—s only
Row 3 (odd)—4 s (10), 6 d (24), 12 s (26)
Row 4 (even)—s only
Row 5 (odd)—5 s (12), 6 d (24), 11 s (24)
Row 6 (even)—s only
Row 7 (odd)—6 s (14), 6 d (24), 10 s (22)
Row 8 (even)—s only
Moving the pattern by more than one twist, perhaps three or five, provides for a more gradual diagonal movement, that is, the slope of the diagonal pattern will be less steep and closer to the horizontal.

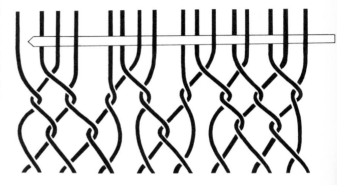

Fig. 8-8. Method 2—large diamonds; moving the double to the left by one single twist in each odd row.

METHOD 3—DIAMONDS

Odd row:

right side:	singles, begin 2/1 and end 1/1
center:	doubles
left side:	singles, begin 1/1 and end 1/2

Even row:

singles only, begin and end 1/1

Method 3 is very similar to Method 1 and is just as versatile. The design can move vertically to make right-angle patterns or it can move diagonally. And, as in Method 1, the structure of the vertical pattern is different from the diagonal structure. The only difference between Methods 1 and 3 is the placement of the row of singles. If you want singles only in an odd row, choose Method 1, and if you want singles only in the even row, use this method.

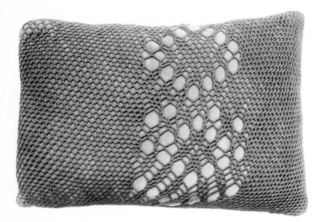

Fig. 8-9. Pillow covering, wool on velvet, Sheila De-metre. Doubles and singles were spranged in the same rows, and an interesting pattern of openings created.

Vertical stripes

In the following pattern, the doubles and singles form vertical stripes. The same number of doubles and singles are spranged in every odd row.

Rows 1 and 2—s only
Row 3 (odd)—7 s (15), 5 d (20), 12 s (25)
Row 4 (even)—s only
Row 5 (odd)—7 s (15), 5 d (20), 12 s (25)
Row 6 (even)—s only

Increasing or decreasing width of vertical stripe

The width of the stripe can be increased or decreased by adding or subtracting one or more doubles on the right, on the left, or on both sides.

In the following example, two doubles (eight threads) are added to the left side of the group of doubles and four singles (eight threads) are subtracted from the left-hand group of singles.

46

Row 7 (odd)—7s (15), 7 d (28), 8 s (17)
Row 8 (even)—s only

Lengthen this stripe by repeating Rows 7 and 8.

In the example below, two doubles are taken from both the left and right sides of the group of doubles. Therefore, four singles are added to both the left- and right-hand groups of singles.

Row 9 (odd)—11 s (23), 3 d (12), 12 s (25)
Row 10 (even)—s only

Moving doubles diagonally

To move the group of doubles diagonally right or left, simply increase one of the groups of singles by an *odd* number of twists and decrease the other by the same odd number of twists. Using an even number would merely continue a pattern of right angles.

In the following example, the pattern is moved to the right by three twists. In every odd row, the group of singles on the right decreases by three twists and the group of singles on the left increases by three twists.

Rows 1 and 2—s only
Row 3 (odd)--15 s (31), 5 d (20), 4 s (9)
Row 4 (even)—s only
Row 5 (odd)—12 s (25), 5 d (20), 7 s (15)
Row 6 (even)—s only
Row 7 (odd) 9 s (19), 5 d (20), 10 s (21)
Row 8 (even)—s only

METHOD 4—FLOATING THREADS

Odd row:
  right side: singles, begin 2/1 and end 1/2
  center: doubles
  left side: singles, begin 2/1 and end 1/2

Even row:
  right side: singles, begin and end 1/1
  center: doubles
  left side: singles, begin and end 1/1

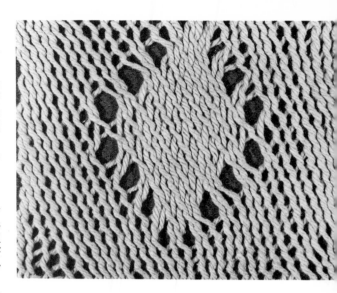

Fig. 8-10. Method 4—floating threads. Doubles and singles are spranged together in every row. Increases to the left and right, and then decreases to the left and right, form a large diamond-shaped area.

This is the first method in which doubles and singles are spranged together in every row. The doubles in one row are split by the doubles in the next. A delicate structure is formed, each of the numerous diamonds filled with two vertical threads. Openings form between the groups of singles and doubles because the first group of singles in the odd row ends 1/2 and the last group of singles begins 2/1.

When moving the pattern of doubles to the right in Method 4, you will have to sprang a "simple twist." This twist is necessary when adjacent threads must be twisted over each other with no thread between the two (fig. 8–11). It only occurs when both doubles and singles are spranged in every row and, at the same time, when both groups of singles in the odd row start 2/1 and end 1/2. After spranging the simple twist, the rest of the single twists on the left are spranged as usual, with one thread between the pair to be twisted. In Method 4 the simple twist is the first twist of the left-hand group of singles in the even row, when the singles on the left are being increased.

The group of doubles is moved diagonally left or right. The vertical threads that run through the diamond shapes float up from the very first row of doubles and do not become twisted until they are picked up as single twists. The group of doubles can also be increased by adding twists or decreased by subtracting twists, as explained in Methods 1–3.

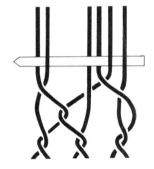

Fig. 8-11. The twist on the left is a simple twist.

Moving doubles diagonally

The doubles can be moved diagonally right or left, while maintaining the same number of doubles. Decrease the group of singles on one side by either two or six threads in every row and increase the group of singles on the other side by the same number of threads. In the following example, the pattern is moved to the right by two threads. The last upper and lower threads of the right-hand singles

become part of the first double (fig. 8-12). The first single twist of the left-hand singles in the even rows is a simple twist.

Rows 1 and 2—s only
Row 3 (odd)—10 s (22), 4 d (16), 10 s (22)
Row 4 (even)—10 s (20), 4 d (16), 12 s (24)
Row 5 (odd)—8 s (18), 4 d (16), 12 s (26)
Row 6 (even)—8 s (16), 4 d (16), 14 s (28)

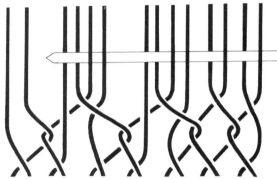

Fig. 8-12. Method 4—floating threads; moving doubles to the right.

To move the doubles to the left by two threads, follow the pattern below. The singles group on the right uses the first upper and lower threads of the first double, and splits it (fig. 8–13).

Rows 1 and 2—s only
Row 3 (odd)—10 s (22), 4 d (16), 10 s (22)
Row 4 (even)—12 s (24), 4 d (16), 10 s (20)
Row 5 (odd)—12 s (26), 4 d (16), 8 s (18)
Row 6 (even)—14 s (28), 4 d (16), 8 s (16)

When moving the doubles to the right by six threads, three upper and three lower threads from the right-hand singles are used in the doubles. Of these six threads, the first two upper and first two lower threads be-

come the first double. The last upper and lower threads become part of the second double. When moving the doubles to the left by six threads, the singles on the right use all of the threads in the first double and the first upper and lower threads in the second double. Moving the pattern by six threads not only creates a more gentle diagonal slope but also forms two slits instead of one between groups of doubles and singles.

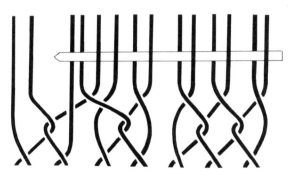

Fig. 8-13. Method 4—floating threads; moving doubles to the left.

Increasing or decreasing doubles

When making the group of doubles wider, the singles must give up four threads for every double added, just as in the previous methods.

In the pattern below, the doubles are increased in both directions at the same time, one double being added in each row. Therefore, instead of taking all four threads from one group of singles, two threads are taken from each of the groups. When the group of doubles is increased in both directions, it grows in a V-shape. In each row, the last upper and lower threads from the singles on the right become part of the first double.

Rows 1 and 2—s only
Row 3 (odd)—13 s (28), 1 d (4), 13 s (28)

Row 4 (even)—13 s (26), 2 d (8), 13 s (26)
Row 5 (odd)—11 s (24), 3 d (12), 11 s (24)
Row 6 (even)—11 s (22), 4 d (16), 11 s (22)
Row 7 (odd)—9 s (20), 5 d (20), 9 s (20)
Row 8 (even)—9 s (18), 6 d (24), 9 s (18)

To finish the V-pattern started above, decrease the doubles in both directions at the same time and the V turns into a diamond (see fig. 8–10). One double is subtracted in every row. Two threads are added to each group of singles in every row, making an addition of two single twists in each odd row.

Row 9 is spranged like Row 7, Row 10 like Row 6, Row 11 like Row 5, and so on. The first group of singles always ends by using one upper and one lower thread from the first double, splitting the double. The second group of singles always begins by using one upper and one lower thread from the last double. In the even rows, the first single on the left side is a simple twist.

You have now finished a simple and elegant diamond design, in fact two of them, as the pattern is repeated in the upper half of the work.

METHOD 5—BROAD RIDGES

Odd row:
- right side: singles, begin 2/1 and end 1/1
- center: doubles
- left side: singles, begin 1/1 and end 1/2

Even row:
- right side: singles, begin and end 1/1
- center: doubles
- left side: singles, begin and end 1/1

Method 5 is very effective because of its broad ridges. Depending on whether the doubles are moved left or right, ridges will be traced on the front or back of the work. Besides being moved diagonally, the group of doubles can be moved vertically, and, in either case, it can be increased or decreased.

The structure of the odd row is the same as in Method 3. However, there are doubles and singles in both odd and even rows in this method.

Moving doubles diagonally

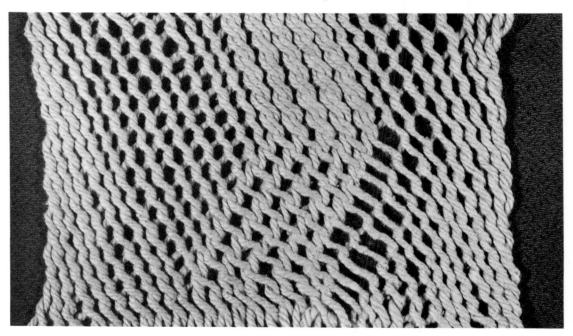

Fig. 8-14. Method 5—broad ridges. The doubles have been moved diagonally first to the left and then to the right.

To move the doubles diagonally, one group of singles must be decreased by either one, three, or five threads and the other groups of singles must be increased by the same number of threads. In the following example, the doubles move to the right by one thread. In every row, the singles on the right decrease by one thread and the singles on the left increase by one thread. The same number of doubles are spranged in every row, although you certainly do not have to adhere to this formula when planning your designs.

When moving the pattern to the right, one upper thread from the singles on the right becomes part of the first double. The lower threads of the doubles are never split (fig. 8–15). This causes the heavy diagonal ridge to form on the back of the piece.

Rows 1 and 2—s only
Row 3 (odd)—10 s (21), 5 d (20), 9 s (19)
Row 4 (even)—10 s (20), 5 d (20), 10 s (20)
Row 5 (odd)—9 s (19), 5 d (20), 10 s (21)
Row 6 (even)—9 s (18), 5 d (20), 11 s (22)

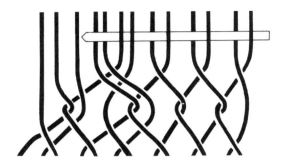

Fig. 8-16. Method 5—broad ridges; moving the doubles to the left. The upper threads of each double do not split.

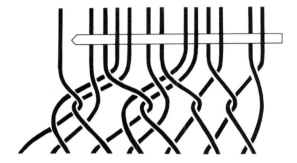

Fig. 8-15. Method 5—broad ridges; moving the doubles to the right. The lower threads of each double do not split.

When moving the pattern to the right by three threads, two upper and one lower thread from the singles on the right are spranged into the first double. When moving the pattern to the right by five threads, three upper and two lower threads from the singles on the right become part of the doubles. The first four of these become the first double. The last upper thread becomes part of the second double.

To move the pattern to the left by three threads, the two lower threads and the first upper thread of the first double are used by the singles on the right. To move the pattern to the left by five threads, the right-hand singles use up all of the threads of the first double and the first lower thread of the second double.

Moving doubles vertically

Method 5 can also be used to make a pattern using right angles instead of diagonal lines.

To move the doubles to the left, the singles on the right must be increased by one, three, or five threads, and the singles on the left decreased by the same number of threads. When moving the pattern to the left by one thread, the singles on the right use the first lower thread from the first double, thereby splitting the lower threads of the first double. The upper threads of the doubles are not split, which causes diagonal ridges to form on the front of the piece (fig. 8–16; see fig. 8–14).

Rows 1 and 2—s only
Row 3 (odd)—10 s (21), 5 d (20), 9 s (19)
Row 4 (even)—11 s (22), 5 d (20), 9 s (18)
Row 5 (odd)—11 s (23), 5 d (20), 8 s (17)
Row 6 (even)—12 s (24), 5 d (20), 8 s (16)

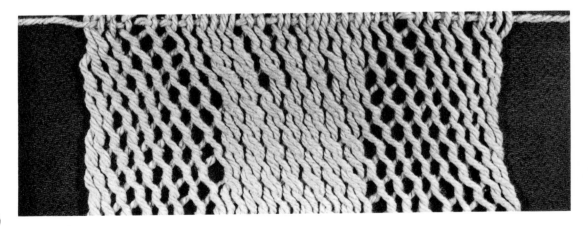

Fig. 8-17. Method 5—broad ridges. The doubles have been moved vertically, without increasing.

This is done by spranging the same number of double twists in every row. One of the groups of singles has the same number of twists in every row but the other group changes, increasing one twist every even row and decreasing one twist every odd row. In the following example, the group of singles on the left always has the same number of twists, as does the group of doubles. The group of singles on the right increases and decreases. Of course this could be reversed so that the left would increase and decrease and the right would remain constant (fig. 8–17).

Rows 1 and 2—*s* only
Row 3 (odd)—7 *s* (15), 7 *d* (28), 8 *s* (17)
Row 4 (even)—8 *s* (16), 7 *d* (28), 8 *s* (16)
Row 5 (odd)—7 *s* (15), 7 *d* (28), 8 *s* (17)
Row 6 (even)—8*s* (16), 7 *d* (28), 8 *s* (16)

Fig. 8-18. Vest, wool, Nancy Dice. Spranged in one piece, using doubles and singles in the same row, the vest has a neck opening of one large slit. The closing was made on either side of the opening at the shoulders, and fringing is tied into the loops.

9 Trebles and Singles

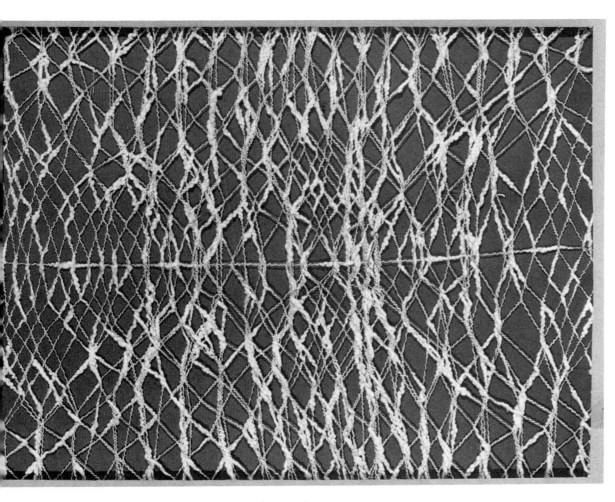

Fig. 9-1. Hanging, cotton bouclé, Lisa Ridenour. An airy effect is created by this pattern of trebles and singles.

By this time you have probably thought of numerous projects you would like to make—wall hangings, clothes, handbags, mats, pillows—and many designs you could incorporate into your projects. Spranging singles and trebles together in the same row will give you one more opportunity for working out these ideas, and the more you add to your techniques, the more creative ideas you will be able to put into form.

Spranging trebles with singles is an extremely versatile technique, unique in that its texture is bulky and its structure very complex. However, this complexity does not mean that using trebles is any more difficult than doubles, but it does create more opportunity for variety.

For ease of learning, the patterns and abbreviations are like those in the last chapter. Sixty warp threads are used, and the number of threads used in the twists is shown in parenthesis. One group of trebles is spranged in the center of a row with a group of singles on each side because, even more so than with doubles, trebles draw in more than singles.

Many of the treble patterns are spranged in the same manner as the corresponding double patterns. In all the methods the trebles move diagonally, and some can form vertical stripes. Once again, the patterns will not provide you with full designs but are enough to get you going.

The terms even and odd are again important when spranging trebles and singles in the same row.

Fig. 9-2. and 9-3. Hangings, rug wool and glass beads, Hella Skowronski. These hangings were made from one warp, which was not spranged in the center, so that it could be cut apart. Cutting the piece leaves long ends for the fringe. The top half looks narrower because of the weight of the beads. Both parts show diagonal ridges created by Method 5—broad ridges.

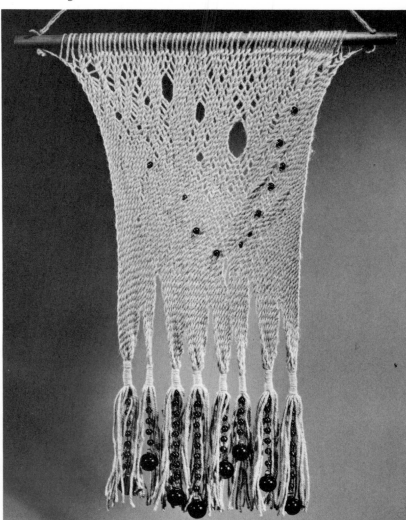

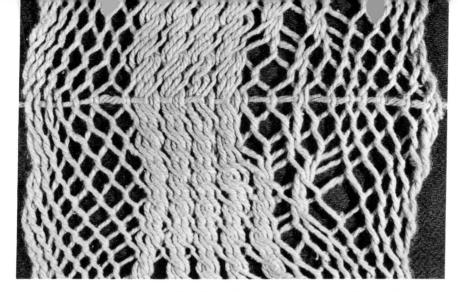

Fig. 9-4. Method 1—diamonds. The trebles have been moved vertically, and decreased on the right.

METHOD 1—DIAMONDS

Odd row:

singles only, begin 2/1 and end 1/2

Even row:

right side: singles, begin and end 1/1
center: trebles
left side: singles, begin and end 1/1

You will find that spranging trebles and singles in the same row is just as versatile as spranging doubles and singles together. In this first method, the treble counterpart of Method 1 in Chapter 8, the trebles can be moved vertically, forming a textured stripe of trebles and a stripe of singles on either side. The different stripes can be warped in different colors if you like, so that structure and color complement each other. The width of the stripe of trebles may be increased or decreased, and you can move the trebles diagonally left or right. The example below moves the trebles vertically and, as you will see, forms a different structure from that formed when the pattern is moved diagonally.

Vertical stripes

Two rows of singles begin each pattern. Since this pattern uses singles only in the odd row, Method 1 actually begins with three rows of singles: an odd, an even, and an odd. The same number of trebles and singles are sprang ed in every even row.

Rows 1, 2, and 3—s only
Row 4 (even)—8 s (16), 5 t (30), 7 s (14)
Row 5 (odd)—s only
Row 6 (even)—8 s (16), 5 t (30), 7 s (14)
Row 7 (odd)—s only

Increasing or decreasing width of vertical stripe

Increases are made as in patterns combining doubles and singles. To increase the group of trebles by one twist, you need *six* threads

(three twists) from the group of singles on the left or right. In the example given below, one treble is added to the right side of the group of trebles, so the group of singles on the right must be decreased by three single twists. To add two treble twists (12 threads), six single twists (12 threads) would have to be subtracted. Of course, the stripe can be widened both to the left and right at the same time.

Row 8 (even)—5 s (10), 6 t (36), 7 s (14)
Row 9 (odd)—s only

To lengthen this stripe, repeat Rows 8 and 9.

Perhaps, instead of increasing the stripe, you would like to have a narrower stripe (fig. 9-4). If so, sprang Rows 10 and 11 as below, applying the same principles in reverse. This example increases the singles on the right by six twists, making two fewer trebles on the right side of the group of trebles.

Row 10 (even)—11 s (22), 4 t (24), 7 s (14)
Row 11 (odd)—s only

Moving trebles diagonally

When the trebles are moved diagonally, the pattern formed is completely different than when they are moved vertically. It is a subtle structure, the threads of the trebles intertwining with the succeeding row of singles.

As with doubles and singles in Method 1 —diamonds, the same number of trebles is spranged in each row while the groups of singles are increased on one side by one, two, four, or five twists, and decreased on the other side by the same number of twists. Decreasing the singles by three or six twists, or any multiple of three, will not move the trebles diagonally but will simply continue a vertical stripe. To move the trebles diagonally to the left reverse all the operations for moving the group to the right.

The example below (see fig. 9–5) decreases the singles on the right by two twists. This provides a more gradual diagonal movement than decreasing by one twist.

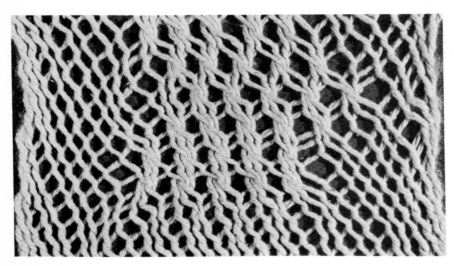

Fig. 9-5. Method 1—diamonds. The trebles have been moved diagonally.

Rows 1, 2, and 3—s only
Row 4 (even)—8 s (16), 5 t (30), 7 s (14)
Row 5 (odd)—s only
Row 6 (even)—6 s (12), 5 t (30), 9 s (18)
Row 7 (odd)—s only

The same number of trebles does not have to be sprangled in every even row. If you wish, you may increase or decrease the width of the trebles area even while moving the pattern diagonally. Follow the directions given on page 44, but remember that each treble uses six threads not four. For example, if you decide to add one treble on the right of the trebles area in Row 6, the row would be sprangled 3 s (6), 6 t (36), 9 s (18).

METHOD 2—LARGE DIAMONDS

Odd row:
    right side: singles, begin 2/1 and end 1/2
    center: trebles
    left side: singles, begin 2/1 and end 1/2

Even row:
    singles only, begin and end 1/1

In this method, the counterpart of Method 2 in Chapter 8, the trebles can be moved diagonally by one, two, four, or five single twists, depending on how steep you want the movement to be. Moving the pattern by three twists produces a completely different but equally interesting pattern of ropes stopped one at a time by the movement of the single twists.

In the example below (see fig. 9–6), the pattern is moved to the left by one twist. In every odd row, the group of singles on the right increases by one twist and the group of singles on the left decreases by one twist. Openings form between each treble and between the groups of trebles and singles.

Rows 1 and 2—s only
Row 3 (odd)—11 s (24), 3 t (18), 8 s (18)
Row 4 (even)—s only
Row 5 (odd)—12 s (26), 3 t (18), 7 s (16)
Row 6 (even)—s only
Row 7 (odd)—13 s (28), 3 t (18), 6 s (14)

Fig. 9-6. Method 2—large diamonds. The trebles have been moved diagonally to the left.

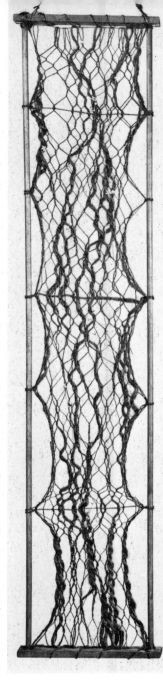

Fig. 9-7. Hanging, thick and thin rayon yarn, Nancy Dice. The pattern is an informal combination of singles and trebles.

METHOD 3—DIAMONDS

Odd row:

right side: singles, begin 2/1 and end 1/1

center: trebles

left side: singles, begin 1/1 and end 1/2

Even row:

singles only, begin and end 1/1

As with Method 3 in Chapter 8, the structure of the twists looks just like Method 1. Which of the methods you choose depends on whether you want to sprang singles in the odd row or the even row. Vertical stripes can be made or the pattern can move diagonally. The stripes can be changed from wide to narrow. Because the single twists immediately on the right and left sides of the trebles are spranged 1/1, no openings form between the groups of singles and trebles, as they did in the previous method.

Fig. 9-8. Method 3—diamonds. The trebles have been moved vertically, while increasing and decreasing.

Vertical stripes

When spranging vertical stripes, the same number of trebles and the same number of singles are spranged in each odd row.

Rows 1 and 2—s only

Row 3 (odd)—9 s (19), 4 t (24), 8 s (17)

Row 4 (even)—s only

Row 5 (odd)—9 s (19), 4 t (24), 8 s (17)

Row 6 (even)—s only

To continue this pattern, repeat Rows 3—6.

Increasing or decreasing width of vertical stripe

Increases and decreases are made in the same manner as previously. Three twists (six threads) must be taken from the group of singles for every treble (six threads) added. In this example, one treble is added on the left by decreasing the number of singles on the left by three twists.

Row 7 (odd)—9 s (19), 5 t (30), 5 s (11)

Row 8 (even)—s only

To narrow the trebles stripe, add three single twists to either group of singles for each treble taken away. In this example, (see fig. 9-8), there are two fewer trebles (12 threads) on the left side, so six singles (12 threads) are added to the left.

Row 9 (odd)—9 s (19), 3 t (18), 11 s (23)

Row 10 (even)—s only

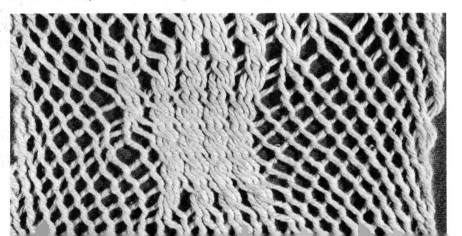

Moving trebles diagonally

To move the trebles diagonally left or right, decrease one group of singles by one, two, four, or five twists and increase the other group of singles by the same number of twists. As before, in Method 1, increasing or decreasing the singles by any multiple of three twists simply continues a vertical stripe.

The pattern below moves the trebles diagonally to the right by two single twists in each group of singles.

Fig. 9-9. *Tangled Web*, fine linen yarn, Sheila Demetre. A combination of twists, seemingly worked at random, creates an intriguing hanging.

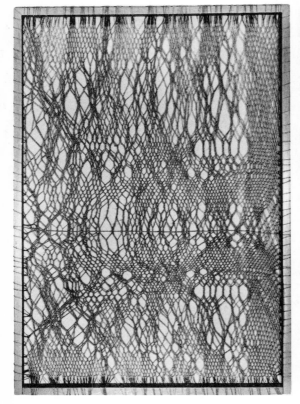

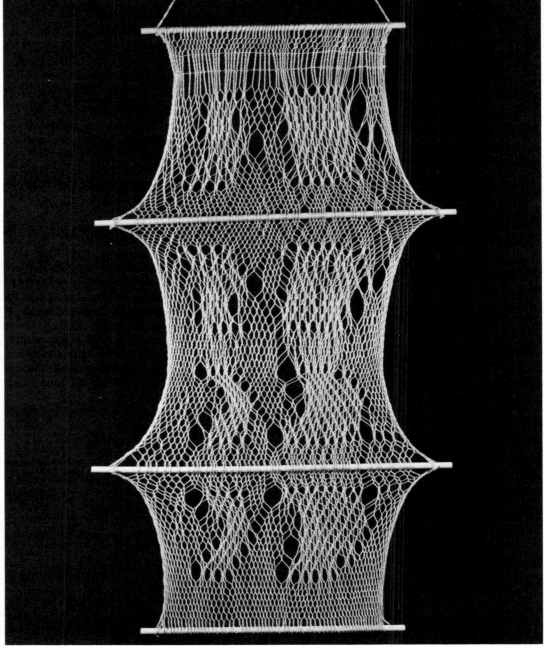

Transit to: Farmha...
Title: Sprang
Item ID: R06876
User name: Irving, Wendy

Transit to: Famil...
Title: Sprana
Item ID: R06876
User name:...

Rows 1 and 2—s only
Row 3 (odd)—9 s (19), 4 t (24), 8 s (17)
Row 4 (even)—s only
Row 5 (odd)—7 s (15), 4 t (24), 10 s (21)
Row 6 (even)—s only

METHOD 4—FLOATING THREADS

Odd row:
    right side: singles, begin 2/1 and end 1/2
    center: trebles
    left side: singles, begin 2/1 and end 1/2

Even row:
    right side: singles, begin and end 1/1
    center: trebles
    left side: singles, begin and end 1/1

This method uses trebles and singles together in every row, as Method 4 in Chapter 8 used doubles and singles. The two-row sequence is followed on both edges of each group of singles. Because the first group of singles in the odd row ends 1/2 and the second group begins 2/1, openings form between the groups of singles and trebles.

The pattern can increase, decrease, and move diagonally by two, four, or any even number of threads in every row. Moving the pattern by two threads makes a steeper incline than moving by four threads.

Fig. 9-10. Hanging, shiny rayon yarn, Hella Skowronski. Worked in two sections, this free-hanging piece is closed in each section by a dowel. Method 4—floating threads—was used.

Moving the pattern by two threads

In the first pattern below, the trebles are moved to the right by two threads, and the same number of trebles are spranged in each row. One upper thread and one lower thread from the singles on the right become part of the first treble (fig. 9–12). One upper thread and one lower thread remain from each treble that has been split to become part of the next treble. The first twist of the left-hand group of singles in each even row is a simple twist.

There will be one floating thread from each treble, which runs vertically one row and is twisted again in the second row. Another floating thread runs two rows and is twisted in the third row. Diagonal ridges, consisting of two threads each, appear on the back of the piece, while short diagonal lines appear on the front. Openings form between the singles and trebles groups, the openings on the left being larger than those on the right. The pattern below is illustrated in Figure 9–11.

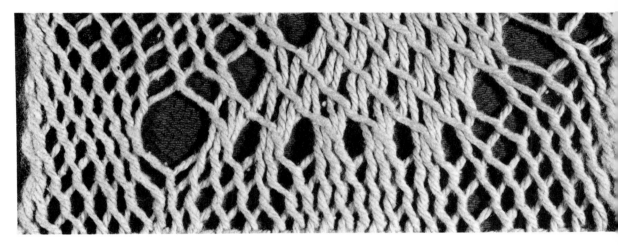

Fig. 9-11. Method 4—floating threads. The trebles have been moved to the right.

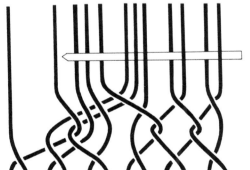

Fig. 9-12. Method 4—floating threads; moving the pattern to the right by two threads in each row.

Rows 1 and 2—*s* only
Row 3 (odd)—7 *s* (16), 5 *t* (30), 6 *s* (14)
Row 4 (even)—7 *s* (14), 5 *t* (30), 8 *s* (16)
Row 5 (odd)—5 *s* (12), 5 *t* (30), 8 *s* (18)
Row 6 (even)—5 *s* (10), 5 *t* (30), 10 *s* (20)

To move the pattern to the left, the first group of singles uses one upper thread and one lower thread from the first treble of the previous row (fig. 9-14). Floating threads and openings are still apparent. However, the diagonal ridges now form on the front of the piece and the short diagonal lines on the back. The pattern below is illustrated in Figure 9–13.

Fig. 9-13. Method 4—floating threads. The trebles have been moved to the left.

Fig. 9-14. Method 4—floating threads; moving the pattern to the left by two threads in each row.

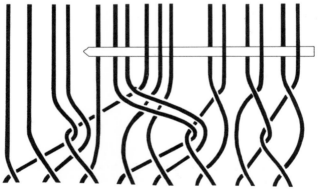

Rows 1 and 2—*s* only
Row 3 (odd)—7 *s* (16), 5 *t* (30), 6 *s* (14)
Row 4 (even)—9 *s* (18), 5 *t* (30), 6 *s* (12)
Row 5 (odd)—9 *s* (20), 5 *t* (30), 4 *s* (10)
Row 6 (even)—11 *s* (22), 5 *t* (30), 4 *s* (8)

Increasing and moving the trebles diagonally (two threads)

To add a treble twist on the right and move the pattern by two threads, the group of singles on the right must decrease by eight threads in every row. This is necessary because the singles on the right must decrease by the same number of threads as are added to both the group of trebles and the singles on the left. The group of singles on the left increases by two threads and the group of trebles increases by six threads (one twist), for a total increase of eight threads. Four upper threads and four lower threads of the right-hand singles group become part of the trebles. The first six of these threads become the first treble.

Rows 1 and 2—*s* only
Row 3 (odd)—13 *s* (28), 2 *t* (12), 9 *s* (20)
Row 4 (even)—10 *s* (20), 3 *t* (18), 11 *s* (22)
Row 5 (odd)—5 *s* (12), 4 *t* (24), 11 *s* (24)
Row 6 (even)—2 *s* (4), 5 *t* (30), 13 *s* (26)

When adding a treble twist on the left side of the group of trebles, and moving the pattern by two threads (see fig. 9–15), the group of singles on the left decreases by eight threads in each row. On the right side, one upper thread and one lower thread from the first treble are used by the singles.

Rows 1 and 2—*s* only
Row 3 (odd)—9 *s* (20), 2 *t* (12), 13 *s* (28)
Row 4 (even)—11 *s* (22), 3 *t* (18), 10 *s* (20)
Row 5 (odd)—11 *s* (24), 4 *t* (24), 5 *s* (12)
Row 6 (even)—13 *s* (26), 5 *t* (30), 2 *s* (4)

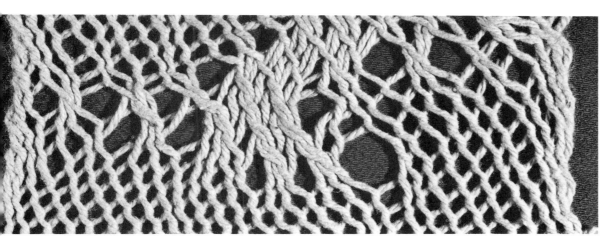

Fig. 9-15. Method 4—floating threads. The trebles have been increased to the left and then to the right.

Moving the pattern by four threads

In the pattern below, the same number of trebles are spranged in each row. When moving the trebles to the right, two upper and two lower threads from the first group of singles are used in the first treble (fig. 9–17).

Fig. 9-16. Method 4—floating threads. The pattern has been moved by four threads to the left and right.

The last two upper and last two lower threads always remain from each treble that has been split, and become part of the next treble. In the even row, the last two upper and last two lower threads of the last treble of the previous row are simple twists.

The appearance is much the same as when the pattern moved by two threads. One thread floats for one row and another floats for two rows. Openings form between the group of trebles and the groups of singles. However, in this pattern the trebles move on a more gradual diagonal, and the diagonal ridges, consisting of two threads each, are on the front of the sprang when the trebles move to the right.

Rows 1 and 2—s only
Row 3 (odd)—9 s (20), 3 t (18), 10 s (22)
Row 4 (even)—8 s (16), 3 t (18), 13 s (26)
Row 5 (odd)—5 s (12), 3 t (18), 14 s (30)
Row 6 (even)—4 s (8), 3 t (18), 17 s (34)
To move the trebles to the left, the singles

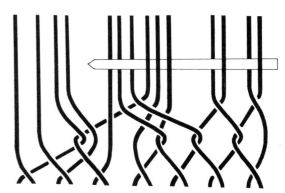

Fig. 9-17. Method 4—floating threads; moving the pattern to the right by four threads in each row.

group on the right takes two upper and two lower threads from the first treble (fig. 9–18).

FIGURE 9-18 . . . .

This leaves one upper thread and one lower thread from each split treble. Again, there are floating threads and openings, but the diagonal ridges are on the back of the piece.

Rows 1 and 2—s only
Row 3 (odd)—9 s (20), 3 t (18), 10 s (22)
Row 4 (even)—12 s (24), 3 t (18), 9 s (18)
Row 5 (odd)—13 s (28), 3 t (18), 6 s (14)
Row 6 (even)—16 s (32), 3 t (18), 5 s (10)

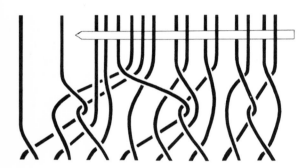

Fig. 9-18. Method 4—floating threads; moving the pattern to the left by four threads in each row.

Increasing and moving the trebles diagonally (four threads)

To increase the trebles, by adding one treble twist on the right, and move the pattern by four threads, the right-hand singles must decrease by ten threads. Since the left-hand singles increase by four threads and the group of trebles increases by six threads (one

twist), the right-hand singles must decrease by the same number of threads, a total of ten. The first six of these become the first treble; the last four become part of the second treble.

Rows 1 and 2—s only
Row 3 (odd)—19 s (40), 2 t (12), 3 s (8)
Row 4 (even)—15 s (30), 3 t (18), 6 s (12)
Row 5 (odd)—9 s (20), 4 t (24), 7 s (16)
Row 6 (even)—5 s (10), 5 t (30), 10 s (20)

To increase the trebles by one on the left and move the pattern by four threads, the singles on the right use two upper and two lower threads from the first treble. The group of singles on the left increases by ten threads.

Rows 1 and 2—s only
Row 3 (odd)—3 s (8), 2 t (12), 19 s (40)
Row 4 (even)—6 s (12), 3 t (18), 15 s (30)
Row 5 (odd)—7 s (16), 4 t (24), 9 s (20)
Row 6 (even)—10 s (20), 5 t (30), 5 s (10)

METHOD 5—BROAD RIDGES

Odd row:

right side:	singles, begin 2/1 and end 1/1
center:	trebles
left side:	singles, begin 1/1 and end 1/2

Even row:

right side:	singles, begin and end 1/1
center:	trebles
left side:	singles, begin and end 1/1

The most apparent difference between this method and Method 4 is that Method 5 does not form openings between the groups. This is always the case when the last twist of the first group of singles and the first twist of the last group of singles are spranged 1/1 in the

odd row, as they were with doubles and singles, Method 5.

The same number of trebles, an increase, or a decrease can be spranged in each row. The pattern can move diagonally right or left by either three, five, or any odd number of threads in each row, depending on whether you want a steep or gentle incline.

Moving the pattern by three threads

When moving the pattern to the right, two upper threads and one lower thread from the right-hand singles are spranged into the first treble (fig. 9–19). The pattern will give you threads that float one row and diagonal ridges, consisting of two threads each, on the back of the piece.

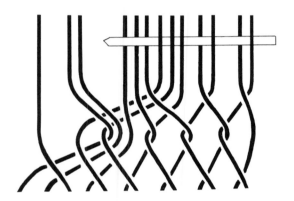

Fig. 9-19. Method 5—broad ridges; moving the pattern to the right by three threads in each row.

Rows 1 and 2—s only
Row 3 (odd)—12 s (25), 3 t (18), 8 s (17)
Row 4 (even)—11 s (22), 3 t (18), 10 s (20)
Row 5 (odd)—9 s (19), 3 t (18), 11 s (23)
Row 6 (even)—8 s (16), 3 t (18), 13 s (26)

To move the trebles to the left, the group of singles on the right takes one upper thread and two lower threads from the first treble (fig. 9–20). The diagonal ridges are on the front of the piece.

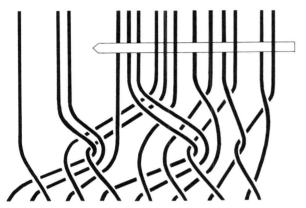

Fig. 9-20. Method 5—broad ridges; moving the pattern to the left by three threads in each row.

Rows 1 and 2—s only
Row 3 (odd)—12 s (25), 3 t (18), 8 s (17)
Row 4 (even)—14 s (28), 3 t (18), 7 s (14)
Row 5 (odd)—15 s (31), 3 t (18), 5 s (11)
Row 6 (even)—17 s (34), 3 t (18), 4 s (8)

Increasing and moving the trebles diagonally (three threads)

To add a treble on the right and move the pattern by three threads, the group of singles on the right must decrease by nine threads. This is because the group of singles on the left increases by three threads and the group of trebles increases by six threads (one twist).

Therefore, the singles on the right must decrease by nine threads. Five upper and four lower threads from the right-hand singles are spranged into the trebles. The first six of these become the first treble. The two upper threads and one lower thread that remain go into the second treble.

Rows 1 and 2—s only
Row 3 (odd)–17 s (35), 2 t (12), 6 s (13)
Row 4 (even)—13 s (26), 3 t (18), 8 s (16)
Row 5 (odd)—8 s (17), 4 t (24), 9 s (19)
Row 6 (even)—4 s (8), 5 t (30), 11 s (22)

To add a treble on the left of the group of trebles and move the pattern by three threads, the group of singles on the right uses one upper and two lower threads from the first treble. The singles on the left decrease by nine threads.

Rows 1 and 2—s only
Row 3 (odd)—6 s (13), 2 t (12), 17 s (35)
Row 4 (even)—8 s (16), 3 t (18), 13 s (26)
Row 5 (odd)—9 s (19), 4 t (24), 8 s (17)
Row 6 (even)—11 s (22), 5 t (30), 4 s (8)

Moving the pattern by five threads

When moving the pattern by five threads to the right, three upper and two lower threads from the singles group on the right are spranged into the first treble. The diagonal is more gentle with five threads than with three. This pattern is different from all other patterns using trebles and singles because the upper threads of each treble are not split. Only the lower threads are split, which gives very strong diagonal ridges on the front of the piece.

Rows 1 and 2—s only
Row 3 (odd)—9 s (19), 3 t (18), 11 s (23)
Row 4 (even)—7 s (14), 3 t (18), 14 s (28)
Row 5 (odd)—4 s (9), 3 t (18), 16 s (33)
Row 6 (even)—2 s (4), 3 t (18), 19 s (38)

When moving the trebles to the left, the singles on the right use all of the lower threads plus two of the upper threads of the first treble. None of the lower threads of the trebles are split, so heavy diagonal ridges form on the back.

Rows 1 and 2—s only
Row 3 (odd)—9 s (19), 3 t (18), 11 s (23)
Row 4 (even)—12 s (24), 3 t (18), 9 s (18)
Row 5 (odd)—14 s (29), 3 t (18), 6 s (13)
Row 6 (even)—17 s (34), 3 t (18), 4 s (8)

Increasing and moving the trebles diagonally (five threads)

To add a treble on the right and move the pattern by five threads, the right-hand singles must decrease by 11 threads. This is because the left-hand singles must increase by five threads and the group of trebles by six threads (one twist). There are six upper and five lower threads from the right-hand singles that become part of the group of trebles. The first six of these make the first treble. The next three upper threads and next two lower threads become part of the second treble.

Rows 1 and 2—s only
Row 3 (odd)—21 s (43), 2 t (12), 2 s (5)
Row 4 (even)—16 s (32), 3 t (18), 5 s (10)
Row 5 (odd)—10 s (21), 4 t (24), 7 s (15)
Row 6 (even)—5 s (10), 5 t (30), 10 s (20)

When adding one treble to the left of the group of trebles and moving the pattern by five threads, the right-hand singles use two upper and three lower threads from the first treble. The left-hand singles decrease by 11 threads.

Rows 1 and 2—s only
Row 3 (odd)—2 s (5), 2 t (12), 21 s (43)
Row 4 (even)—5 s (10), 3 t (18), 16 s (32)
Row 5 (odd)—7 s (15), 4 t (24), 10 s (21)
Row 6 (even)—10 s (20), 5 t (30), 5 s (10)

GREATER INCREASES
OR DECREASES

Of course, you can increase or decrease the group of trebles by more than one twist and move the pattern diagonally at the same time. Follow the directions on page 44, but remember that each treble uses six threads, not four. It is easy to determine how to sprang the row if you answer two questions. First, how many threads have been added to or subtracted from one of the groups of singles in order to move the pattern diagonally? Second, how many threads have been added to or subtracted from the group of trebles? When increasing, one group of singles must decrease by the same number of threads added to the other group of singles and the trebles group (or the combination of the two). For example, if you move the pattern to the left by two threads and add one treble (six threads) on the left, the singles on the left must decrease by eight threads. When decreasing, extra singles must be added in the same way.

Singles, doubles, and trebles

As you make your projects using combinations of twists, you do not have to sprang only doubles and singles or only trebles and singles. Doubles also combine nicely with trebles and all three types of twists together make fascinating designs. Experiment with what you have learned, and you will find yourself well rewarded. Simply remember that any time you use all three twists, your warp should be set up in multiples of twelve.

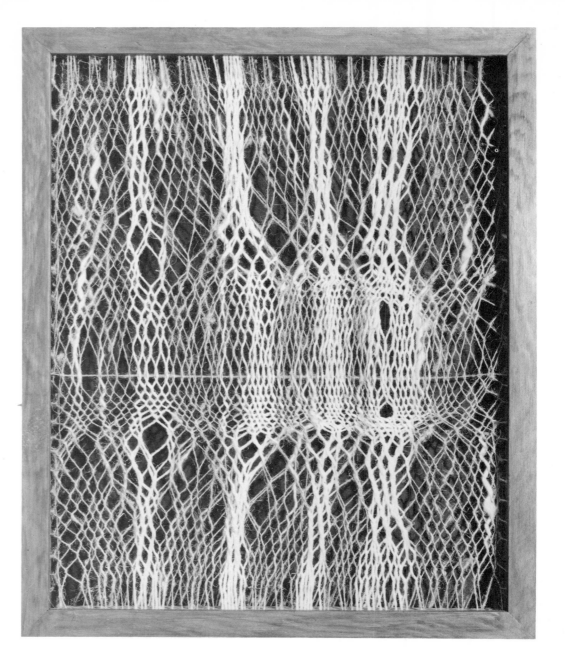

Fig. 9-21. Hanging, textured linen yarn, Hella Skowronski. The trebles, worked in off-white, lead the eye to the center of singles, where the combination with natural-colored yarn gives the effect of swaying movement.

10 Z Twist

The Z twist brings new depth and dimension into your work. So far, structure, color, and texture have been the important forces in your sprang. These are certainly still important, but the Z twist adds the subtle use of movement and light, so that numerous forces play on and within the sprang.

The upper thread in the Z twist moves to the right, directing the eye in that direction. The upper thread in the S twist moves to the left, leading the eye to the left. When the two twists are combined, the sprang takes on a new kind of activity. This can either be pronounced, as in the cone hanging in Figures 10–2 and 10–3 or very understated, as in the hanging in Figure 10-12.

So far, you have used the S twist in all of the twists you have learned. It is a simple matter to transfer this knowledge to the Z twist. In fact, any of the patterns can be spranged using one twist or the other. Although you have not spranged it yet yourself, every piece you have done contains the Z twist, since a Z twist is formed in the top half of the sprang when an S twist is spranged in the bottom half. When spranging a Z twist, an S twist will be formed on top.

Fig. 10-2 and 10-3. Cone hanging and detail, synthetic raffia, Lisa Ridenour. Rows of S and Z twists produce a dynamic feeling of motion.

Fig. 10-1. Handbag, textured wool, Sylvia Tacker. This is done in singles only, with a decorative touch of Z twists at the bottom. The drawstring is threaded through the loops, and the closing is done by looping, for strength.

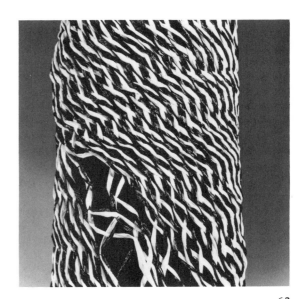

MAKING THE TWIST

Making the Z twist differs from making the S twist in four ways.

1. The upper thread is pushed down before the lower thread is picked up.

2. The upper thread moves to the right of the lower thread in a twist.

3. One *lower* thread is between the pair to be twisted.

4. The odd row starts two down, one up (*2/1*) and ends one down, two up (*1/2*). In the Z-twist instructions, the numerical abbreviations give the threads to be pushed down first. To differentiate these instructions from S twists, the numerical abbreviations designating Z twists will be *italicized*. For example, *2/1* is read as a Z twist that is made two down and one up.

You may find it easier and more practical to pick up the threads with your fingers than with the pick-up stick. The lower thread to the left of the twist just made has a tendency to be hidden behind the twist. When you use your fingers, you can prevent this thread from getting lost by pulling the twisted threads to the right, making the lower thread visible.

Later, you will see how to sprang a row of Z twists after a row of S twists. But for now, it is easiest to learn the Z twist if you start with a new warp, one on which you have not done any S twists.

SINGLE Z TWIST

The Z twist follows the same two-row sequence as the S twist. Rows 1, 3, 5, etc. are spranged as odd rows. Rows 2, 4, 6, etc. are spranged as even rows. For the directions that begin on page 68, use a warp of 40 threads.

Odd row

1. Push the first two upper threads to the right of the first lower thread (fig. 10–4).

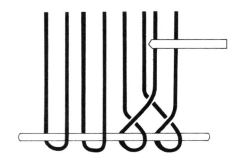

Fig. 10-4. Beginning the first Z twist in an odd row.

2. Push the two upper threads down and pick up the first lower thread (fig 10–5). *Two upper threads are always pushed down in the first twist in the odd row.*

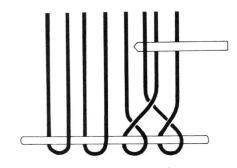

Fig. 10-5. Completing the first Z twist in an odd row.

3. Push the next upper thread to the right and down.

4. Pick up the next lower thread (fig. 10–6).

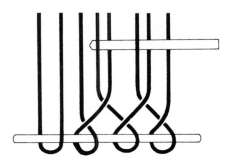

Fig. 10-6. Completing the second Z twist in an odd row.

5. Continue across the row in this manner.

6. End the row by pushing the last upper thread to the right and down and picking up the last two lower threads (fig. 10–7).

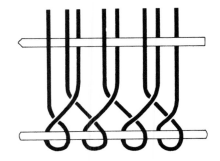

Fig. 10-7. Odd row of Z twists completed.

As usual, transfer the twists to the transfer stick. Instead of pushing the tip of the stick under the warp, leave it on top, pointed up and away from the work area. As you remember, the next lower thread to be spranged tends to lose itself behind the twists. Leaving the tip of the transfer stick on top of the warp makes this lower thread visible.

Even row

1. Push the first upper thread to the right of the first lower thread.

2. Push the upper thread down and pick up the first lower thread (fig. 10–8). *Only one upper thread is pushed down in the first twist in an even row.*

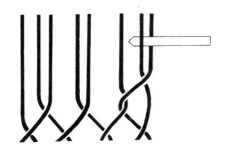

Fig. 10-8. Completing the first Z twist in an even row.

3. Push the next upper thread to the right and down.

4. Pick up the next lower thread (fig. 10–9).

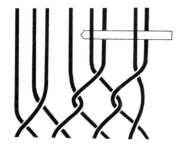

Fig. 10-9. Completing the second Z twist in an even row.

5. Continue across the row.

6. End the row by pushing the last upper thread to the right and down and pulling up the last lower thread (fig. 10–10).

Row 3, an odd row, is like Row 1. Row 4, even, is like Row 2.

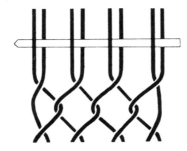

Fig. 10-10. Even row of Z twists completed.

Double and treble Z twists

So far, you have used the Z twist to sprang singles. However, the technique of pushing the upper thread to the right and picking up the lower thread can be used with slits, doubles, and trebles. Try some of these other twists, explained in Chapters 5, 6, 7, 8, and 9, using the Z twist. It is just as easy as the S twist, isn't it?

S AND Z IN SEPARATE ROWS

The Z twist can be spranged alone but is extremely effective in combination with the S twist. Since the S twist moves from right to left, and the Z twist moves from left to right, a zig-zag appearance is achieved. Light becomes an important and integral part of the sprang itself, as it reflects and intensifies this movement.

Combine the two types of twists, first using only one type across a full row. Each type of twist must be spranged for an even number of rows, and the change is always made in an odd row.

When you change from a row of S to a row of Z or from Z to S, only simple twists are made. That is, there is no thread between the pair to be twisted; the upper and lower threads are next to each other. When you sprang the even row following the change, the twists in the odd row will look like x's. If you sprang one type of twist for more than two rows, the simple twist shows up only in the odd row in which the change is made.

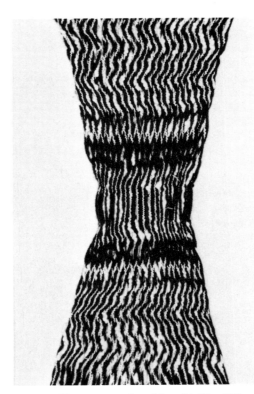

Fig. 10-11. Hanging, wool and bouclé, Lisa Ridenour. The optical movement is achieved by alternating light and dark colors in rows of S and Z twists.

Row 1 (odd singles, S twist): begin 2/1, end 1/2

Row 2 (even singles, S twist): begin 1/1, end 1/1

Row 3 (odd singles, Z twist): begin *2/1*, end *1/2*

Remember that the Z twists are shown in *italic*, the threads to be pushed *down* given first. In this row the threads to be twisted are next to each other, so simple twists are spranged.

Row 4 (even singles, Z twist): begin *1/1*, end *1/1*

In this row, there is again one lower thread between each pair to be twisted. The twists in Row 3 now look like x's.

Row 5 (odd singles, S twist): as Row 1
Only simple twists are made.

Row 6 (even singles, S twist): as Row 2
There is one upper thread between the pair to be twisted. The twists in Row 5 now look like x's.

Continue the two-row sequence of S and Z twists as long as you like. It is especially interesting to sprang this pattern with two warp colors, alternating color every other warp thread. The result is narrow, horizontal stripes. See pages 18 and 76 to learn how to warp a sprang using two colors.

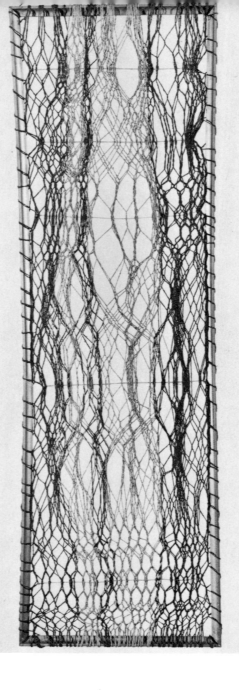

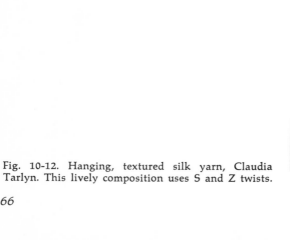

Fig. 10-12. Hanging, textured silk yarn, Claudia Tarlyn. This lively composition uses S and Z twists.

S AND Z IN THE SAME ROW

The S and Z twists can also be spranged within the same row.

Row 1 (odd, S): begin 2/1, end 1/2
      (odd, Z): begin *2/1*, end *1/2*

Because each group of either S or Z begins and ends with three threads in each twist, a slit forms between the groups. In the odd row, four threads next to each other are down at the point of change from S to Z (fig. 10–14). When changing from Z to S, four threads next to each other are up.

Row 2 (even, S): begin 1/1, end 1/1
      (even, Z): begin *1/1*, end *1/1*

In the even row, the opening at the point of change appears. This slit is closed by the following odd row.

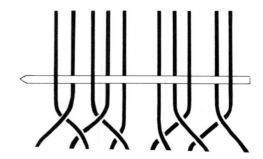

Fig. 10-14. Detail of an odd row with both S and Z twists. The point of change is from S (the group on the right) to Z (the group on the left).

Fig. 10-13. Hanging, wool, Hella Skowronski. S and Z twists spranged in the same row create strong movement. Slits form at the points of change, creating a pattern of their own.

Each group of S or Z moves diagonally left or right. The width of a group may remain the same in every row or the number of threads may be increased or decreased. Always increase or decrease in the odd row. You may wish to change the direction of movement by switching a group of S to a group of Z, or Z to S, and, as previously mentioned, this also must be done in the odd row. If you have not yet warped your loom, set up now with 40 threads.

Fig. 10-15. Pillow cover, thick and thin wool and rayon used as one strand, velvet, Hella Skowronski. S and Z twists are spranged in the same row.

Moving the pattern to the right

The groups of S and Z, all spranged in single twists, are moved by an even number of threads in every odd row. Depending on how gentle or severe you want the diagonal movement to be, this could be two, four, six, or more threads. In the pattern below, the center group of Z twists always uses the same number of threads and is moved to the right by two threads in every odd row. The S group on the right decreases by two threads in every odd row and the S group on the left increases by two threads.

When moving a group of S or Z to the right by two threads, one upper and one lower thread from one group become part of the next group. When moving a group by four threads, two upper threads and two lower threads are spranged into the next group, and when moving by six threads, three upper threads and three lower threads go into the next group. The same number of threads is spranged in each group in the even row as in the previous odd row.

Rows 1 and 2—S only
Row 3 (odd)—6 S (14), 7 Z (16), 4 S (10)
Row 4 (even)—7 S (14), 8 Z (16), 5 S (10)
Row 5 (odd)—5 S (12), 7 Z (16), 5 S (12)
Row 6 (even)—6 S (12), 8 Z (16), 6 S (12)

Moving the pattern to the left

To move the pattern to the left by two threads, each group of S or Z uses one upper and one lower thread from the next group. If you move the pattern by four threads, two upper and two lower threads from the next group would be used. Just as when moving the pattern to the right, each group in the even row uses the same number of *threads* as in the odd row immediately preceding it.

Row 7 (odd)—6 S (14), 7 Z (16), 4 S (10)
Row 8 (even)—7 S (14), 8 Z (16), 5 S (10)
Row 9 (odd)—7 S (16), 7 Z (16), 3 S (8)
Row 10 (even)—8 S (16), 8 Z (16), 4 S (8)

Increasing or decreasing

A group of S or Z may be increased or decreased by an even number of threads every odd row. The following example, all spranged in singles, increases the Z area on the right and the S area in the center by adding four threads to each group in every odd row. The Z area on the left decreases by eight threads in every odd row.

Rows 1 and 2—S only
Row 3 (odd)—5 Z (12), 5 S (12), 7 Z (16)
Row 4 (even)—6 Z (12), 6 S (12), 8 Z (16)
Row 5 (odd)—7 Z (16), 7 S (16), 3 Z (8)
Row 6 (even)—8 Z (16), 8 S (16), 4 Z (8)
Row 7 (odd)—9 Z (20), 9 S (20)
Row 8 (even)—10 Z (20), 10 S (20)

The rest of the pattern decreases the Z group on the right and the S group in the center by subtracting four threads in every odd row.

Row 9 (odd)—7 Z (16), 7 S (16), 3 Z (8)
Row 10 (even)—8 Z (16), 8 S (16), 4 Z (8)
Row 11 (odd)—5 Z (12), 5 S (12), 7 Z (16)
Row 12 (even)—6 Z (12), 6 S (12), 8 Z (16)

Although the patterns in this chapter have been given in single twists, you can easily adapt them to double or treble twists by reworking the number of threads in each stripe —doubles use four threads, trebles use six. Variations can also be made by spranging different twists in different directions. For example, singles in S, doubles in Z, singles in S in the same row. Experiment, and see what happens.

Fig. 10-16. Hanging, silk yarn, Hella Skowronski. S and Z twists in the same row create a graceful circular motion.

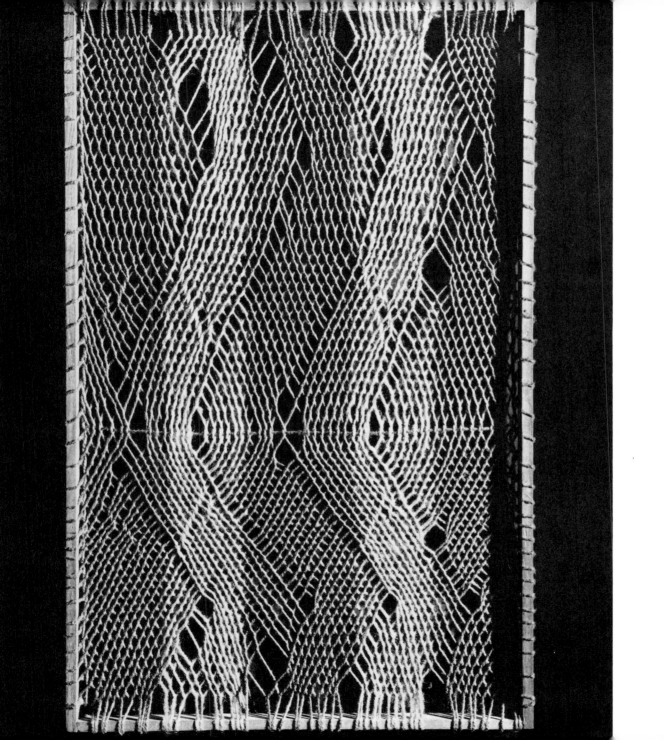

11 Spranging in Sections—Stopping the Twist

Until recently, spranging large pieces with numerous designs has been somewhat difficult. But now sprang limits you neither in size nor design. Do you want a long warp? Use the continuous warp. Do you want to sprang more than one design in the same piece? Use a stop cord to divide the sprang into sections. Each section may have a different design, or one design can be continued through the sections. As far as we know, we have originated this method of using a stop cord to sprang in sections.

Although this technique can be used on a regular warp, it is especially handy to know how to stop the twist when using a continuous warp, which was described in Chapter 3. Of course, you could push every row of twists around the frame to the bottom of the movable dowel. However, if you use a stop cord and sprang only a portion of the warp at a time, you can skip this rather tedious task. The twist need only be pushed to the stop cord.

Each portion of warp worked at one time is a section. Like a complete work in itself, each section has a top and bottom and a closing row. A stop cord is used to end one section and begin the next. It literally stops the twist at any point you choose in the warp. A stop cord is nothing more than a long cord of a different color than the shed cords, to avoid confusing them.

As you know, when you sprang S twists, Z twists are formed in the top half of your work. In the same way, when spranging S twists in the first section of your warp, Z twists will form in the upper half of the same section. In the second section, you will sprang Z twists, as a continuation of the Z twists in the upper half of the first section.

Fig. 11-1. Hanging, wool and brass tubing, Marjorie Moore. Spranged in three sections, with brass tubing in stop sheds, the piece has a formal appearance.

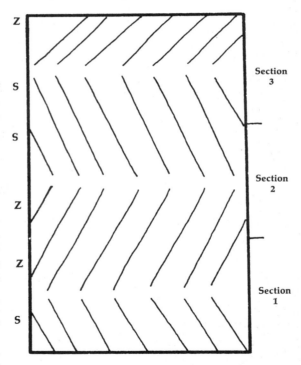

Fig. 11-2. A warp spranged in sections. The twist in the last half of one section is continued to the first half of the next.

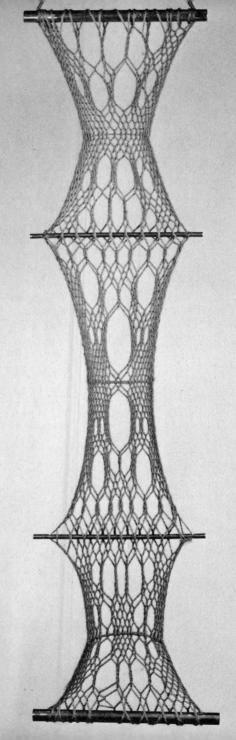

Since Z twists continue from the center of the first section to the center of the second section, you may continue an uninterrupted design through the sections if you wish.

Follow the directions in Chapter 3 for setting up a continuous warp. Make the warp as wide as you want for your design and as long as the frame or loom allows. This chapter will describe a sprang with three sections, using both S and Z twists. Only the construction of the sections will be explained —the designs are your own!

Section 1

1. Put the shed stick and the stop cord into the shed formed by the movable dowel. The first thread is on top of the shed stick.

2. Push the cord up the warp to the place you want the first section to end. The shed in which the cord has been placed is called the stop shed. It ends the first section and begins the second. When the piece is finished, the stop shed will not show. Each section does not necessarily have to be one-third the length of the total warp, as it is in Figure 11–2. Make this first section as long or as short as you want, but not so short that you don't have room to work. Also it is easier to work if the stop cord is not pushed up so far that it goes over the top of the frame to the back.

3. Be sure to tie the stop cord to the sides of the frame.

4. Sprang odd and even rows of singles, using S twists. Push these rows to the bottom and to the top, next to the stop cord, and insert shed cords to secure the twists, just as before. The first row of singles will not twist on top below the stop cord until the second row has been spranged.

5. Finish the first section, using S twists.

6. Close the center of the first section.

7. Put a shed stick and shed cord into the

stop shed. Like all shed cords, this shed cord will eventually be removed. Move the stop cord to the end of the second section, wherever you want that to be, leaving it in the same shed. You may have to move the continuous warp down (see directions on page 21).

It is important to know two things about the stop shed to determine how to continue in the second section. First, is it an odd or even row? Second, is it spranged in S or Z twists?

Remember that the first row was odd, and this was pushed up to the stop cord. Therefore, the first row on the bottom and the first row on the top are both odd.

As you know, the twist that forms in the top half of the piece is opposite that spranged in the bottom half. Since the bottom half was spranged with S twists, the top half, including the stop shed, is in Z twists.

Check the stop shed. On the right side, there are two threads down and one up (2/1) and on the left side one thread down and two up (1/2). This combination has to be an odd row of Z twists.

Section 2

Following the two-row sequence, the first row of the second section must be even. Z twists are spranged in Section 2 as a continuation of the top half of Section 1.

1. Sprang an even row of singles, using Z twists. Row 1 will not twist below the new stop shed. Row 2 will form the twist on top.

2. Finish the second section, using Z twists and close the center.

3. Put a shed stick and shed cord into the stop shed. Remove the stop cord, as it is not necessary in the last section, since the twist is stopped by the dowel at the end of the warp.

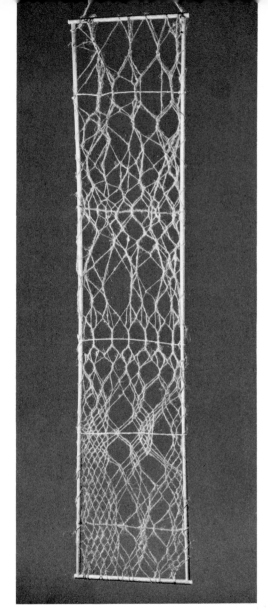

Fig. 11-3. Hanging, handspun linen, Claudia Tarlyn. The see-through effect of this delicate piece would be enhanced by placing it in a window.

71

The first row in the second section was even, making the stop shed even also. Because the bottom half was spranged with Z twists, the top half forms S twists. Therefore, the stop shed is an even row of S. This is also indicated by the fact that the selvedge of the stop shed is one up and one down (1/1).

Section 3

Since the stop shed was even, the first row of the third section must be odd. The S twist is used as a continuation of the top half of the second section. Beginning with an odd row of S, the third section is spranged just like the first.

1. Sprang an odd row, using S twists. Again, the first row does not twist at the top; the second row forms a twist.

2. Finish the third section, using S twists, and close the center.

You can sprang as many sections as your warp and design allow. The first row of the fourth section would be just like the first row of the second section, and so on. However, remember to leave the stop cord in place until the last section. After you complete a piece on a continuous warp, the movable dowel must be removed to open the sprang into one long piece. See Chapter 14 for finishing methods.

In the method described above, the first row of each section was spranged in singles. This row can be spranged in doubles instead. In Section 1, all twists in the first row, including the first and last, would be spranged 2/2. In Section 2, the doubles would begin and end 1/1. In Section 3, the doubles would begin and end 2/2.

After completing the first two rows of a section, you might certainly finish the section using a combination of S and Z twists, as explained previously.

Review

Here are the points to remember about stopping the twist and starting a new section when singles are spranged in the first row of each section.

1. If the stop shed is odd, begin the new section with an even row.

2. If the stop shed is even, begin the new section with an odd row.

3. Alternate spranging S and Z twists every other section.

4. Vary the length of the sections to add interest.

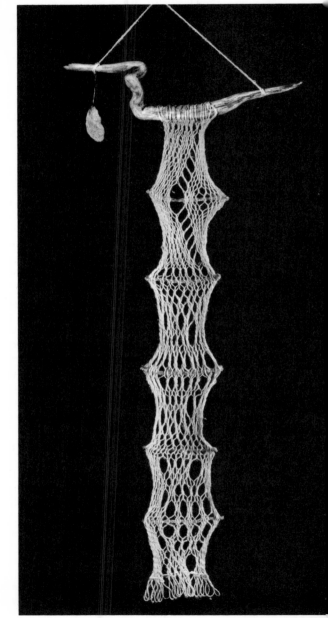

Fig. 11-4. Hanging, linen, natural wood, shell, Aves Pickering. This is spranged in three sections with stop sheds and closings held by pipe cleaners.

12 Spranging in Sections—Changing the Twist

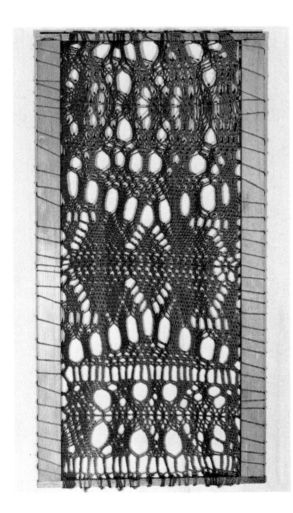

Fig. 12-1. Hanging, cotton yarns, Marney Chapman. S and Z twists are apparent in this closely set warp.

By alternately spranging S and Z twists with the use of a stop cord, you learned in the last chapter how to sprang longer and more varied pieces. In this chapter you will learn how to take advantage of this method so that the sprang appears quite different from any of your previous work. It is done very simply by spranging S twists, or Z twists, in all of the sections. We call it changing the twist (even though you sprang the same twist) because the direction of the twists automatically changes at the stop cord.

The opposing left and right movements of the S and Z twists are very pronounced, lights and shadows playing on the sprang and intensifying the effect. This visual movement joins with the twist structure and the structure of the sections to form extremely appealing designs.

In the stop twists you have just learned, the stop shed in the completed work was not apparent because the same twist direction was continued from one section to the next. For example, if you spranged S twists in Section 1, Z twists formed on top, and the Z twist was continued by spranging it at the bottom of Section 2.

In the change-twist method, the twist is not continued from one section to the next. When only S twists are spranged, Z twists form in the top half of each section. If you start with S twists in the next section, the direction of the twist changes from the Z on the top half to S in the new section. If you choose to sprang only Z twists, S twists form in the top half, and to sprang Z twists in the

following section will change the twist from S to Z (fig. 12-2). When the twist is changed from the top half of one section to the bottom half of the next, the stop shed is very apparent, showing up as the point at which the twists change direction.

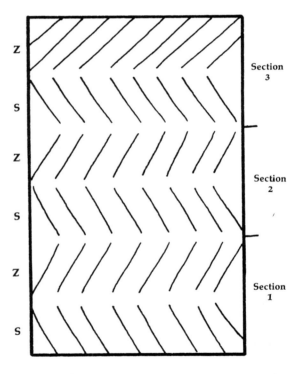

Fig. 12-2. The first half of each section is always spranged in the same twist direction.

CHANGING FROM Z TO S

The directions given below should be simple to follow, as they build upon what you have learned in Chapter 11. Although directions are given for a continuous warp, you can sprang in sections by stopping and changing the twists on a frame loom, as long as it is large enough to leave you room to work in each section.

Section 1

1. Insert the shed stick and the stop cord into the shed formed by the movable dowel.

2. Push the stop cord to where you want the first section to end, and tie the cord to the sides of the frame. The stop cord ends the first section and begins the second.

3. Sprang S twists, beginning with an odd row. This produces Z twists in the top half of the section. There will be no twist below the stop cord. As in all of the sections, the second row will form the twist on top. Since the first row is an odd row of S, the stop shed is an odd row of Z.

Section 2

1. Sprang an even row of Z twists. This is a continuation of the last half of the first section, as the two-row sequence must be finished. There will be no twist below the stop cord.

2. Sprang an odd row of S twists. The threads will cross, not twist, both at the bottom and top, as there is no thread between the pair being spranged.

3. Sprang an even row of S twists. The threads will now twist below the stop cord.

4. Continue the design with S twists and close the center. Since the section began with an even row of Z, the stop shed should logically be an even row of S. However, this stop

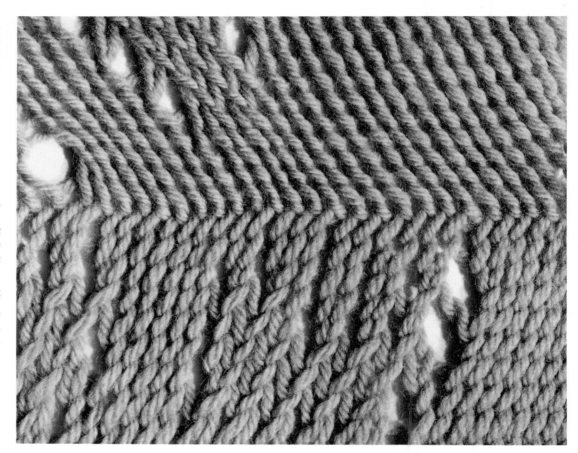

Fig. 12-3. Detail of poncho in Figure 8-1. A dramatic change of direction is possible when changing from Z to S twists.

shed does not fit the rule. On the right side, there is one upper thread not in the twist, and one lower thread and one upper thread twisted (fig. 12–4). On the left side, there is one upper thread and one lower thread twisted, and one lower thread not in the twist. The untwisted threads on the edges will be twisted in the first row of Section 3.

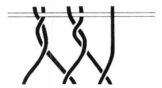

Fig. 12-4. The right side of the stop shed when changing from Z to S twists, in Section 2.

74

Section 3

1. All of the threads are now in order for the odd row. Sprang an odd row of S. There will be no twist below the stop cord.

2. Finish the section using the S twist, and close the center.

Since the first row of the section was an odd row of S, the stop shed is an odd row of Z. This stop shed is just like Section 1.

If continuing for more than three sections, Section 4 would be like Section 2 and Section 5 would be like Section 3.

CHANGING FROM S TO Z

Section 1

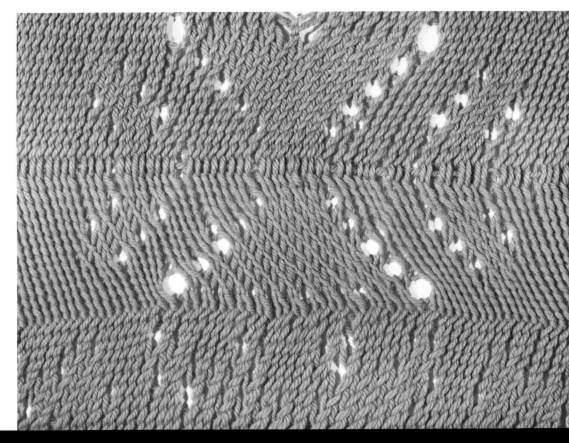

Sprang Z twists, starting with an odd row. There is no twist below the stop cord until the second row. Since the first row is an odd row of Z twists, the stop shed is an odd row of S twists.

Section 2

1. Sprang an even row of S twists. This must be done to finish the two-row sequence, as an even row puts the threads back in order. This row does not twist below the stop cord.

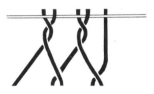

Fig. 12-5. Detail of poncho in Figure 8-1. A change from Z twists in one section to S twists in the next is apparent at the bottom of the photograph. The closing in the center shows the change from S to Z within one section.

2. Sprang an odd row of Z twists. The threads will cross, rather than twist, at the top and bottom because there is no thread between the pair being spranged. The first and last threads of the row will not seem to cross with another thread after spranging.

3. Sprang an even row of Z twists. This row will form the twist. The first and last threads are now in the twist and all of the threads are back in order.

4. Finish the section using Z twists. Close the center.

The stop shed should be an even row of Z, since the first row was an even row of S. However, this is not the case. On the right side of the stop shed, one lower thread is not in the twist, and one upper thread and one lower thread are twisted (fig. 12–6). On the left side, there is one upper thread and one lower thread twisted, and one upper thread is not in the twist. The loose threads which were not in the twist will be twisted in the first row of Section 3.

Fig. 12-6. The right side of the stop shed in section two when changing from S to Z twists.

Section 3

1. Sprang an odd row of Z twists. There is no twist on top until the second row.

2. Finish the section, using the Z twist, and close the center.

Since the first row was an odd row of Z, the stop shed is an odd row of S, just as in Section 1. If continuing, Section 4 is spranged like Section 2, and Section 5 like 1 and 3.

13 Full Twist

Fig. 13-1. Pajama string from Pakistan. The full twist is used to achieve a geometric design. (Collection of Jeannette Lund; photo by Kent Kammerer.)

You have learned to sprang numerous patterns using the three basic twists. Most of the patterns described have been structural ones, although sprang also is capable of producing beautiful color patterns. Perhaps you have already combined more than one color in your warps, making stripes of varying widths. Another method offering numerous possibilities uses a warp with two alternating colors, the colors changing every other thread. The pattern is developed using the full twist.

Chapter 10 described how to make horizontal color stripes by spranging S twists for two rows followed by Z twists for two rows. With the full twist, you can produce even more variations, such as blocks of color and patterns of solid color. This is most effective with a closely set warp.

SETTING UP

It is not difficult to warp two colors at once. Tie both colors to the top dowel at the same time. Keeping one finger between the two threads to separate them and to keep the tension on both threads even, warp as usual. The same color is always to the right, the other, to the left. For convenience when learning, use one distinctly light color and one distinctly dark color. The color of the thread on the left edge of the finished warp will be the opposite of the one on the right edge. Warp 60 threads, 30 of each color.

Before spranging, all of the threads of one of the colors must be brought up, to the front. The color of the first upper thread is brought forward. Using a shed stick, pick up, but do not twist, all of the threads of this color. Begin by picking up the first upper thread on the right. For example, if the color to be brought forward is light, pick up all of the light threads from between the dark ones. Some of the threads picked up will be on top of the dowel, others will come from below the dowel. When you have finished, all of the threads of one color will be on top of the shed stick, all of the other color below. Put shed cords into the shed, and push one to the

top and the other to the bottom. Push the shed stick to the top of the warp.

Sprang an odd row of S. You may find it more difficult than normal to pick up the threads in this first row. The row will not at first appear as neat on the dowel as you are used to because some of the upper threads originally come from behind the dowel and vice versa. Pick up the first two threads of the "lower" color. Push down the first thread of the "upper" color. Then, in alternating order:

1. Pick up the next thread of the "lower" color.

2. Push down the next thread of the "upper" color.

3. Repeat along the row. The last twist will be 1/2, as previously.

If all of the light threads were up before, now all of the dark threads will be up.

MAKING THE TWIST

Sprang a full twist by first making the regular single twist. When using the S twist, the thread which was up is now down and to the left. Bring this thread under and to the right of the upper thread and then up. If you were making regular Z twists, the top thread would go down to the right and back up to the left. In either S or Z, the thread that was up in the first place is again up (fig. 13–2). As an example, assume the upper thread is dark and the lower thread light. Spranging a regular twist brings up the light thread. Completing the full twist brings the dark thread up again. Because you twist the same two threads around each other, you will find it easier to use your fingers than the pick-up stick.

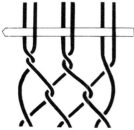

Fig. 13-2. The two twists on the left are full twists. A "point of change" is between the first and second twists on the right.

The full twist can be spranged in the odd or even row, using S or Z twists. However, it can never be spranged on the first or last twists of the row. In other words, you can never sprang a complete row of full twists. In the directions that follow in this chapter "full twist only" should be understood as *full twists except for the first and last twist.* If the first and last twists in the odd row were full twists, your threads would not be in working order for the even row. Full twists will be designated by *f* and regular twists by *r*.

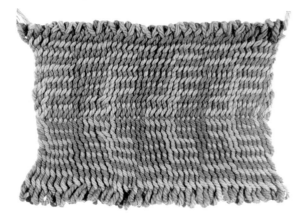

Fig. 13-3. Mat, bulky wool, Hella Skowronski. Two colors were warped alternately and spranged with full twists.

BLOCKS OF COLOR, OR "MIXED-COLOR" TWISTS

All of the upper threads in your warp are of one color and all of the lower threads are of the other color. Using either the S or Z twist, sprang two or three rows of regular twists only. Each row will bring up the opposite color, forming thin bands of color. For example, if light threads are picked up in the first row, dark threads will be picked up in the second row. This is most evident and most effective when the warp threads are tightly pushed together.

More than one block of color can be brought up in each row by using both the regular and the full twist. If the upper threads in the previous row were light, regular twists will bring up dark threads, but full twists will bring up light threads again. By combining the dark or light threads you can produce various color patterns.

In the example below, only the rows that use both full and regular twists are called pattern rows. The pattern row can be either odd or even. However, it is easier to plan a pattern in advance if the pattern row is even, since all of the twists there are spranged 1/1.

In the pattern row below, the first ten twists are regular, the second ten are full, and the third ten are regular. This accounts for 60 threads.

Row 1 (odd)—*r* only
Since all of the threads brought up in Row 1 are the same color, you have made a single-color horizontal stripe.
Row 2 (even)—10 *r*, 10 *f*, 10 *r*
Row 2 produces three blocks of color in the horizontal stripe.
Row 3 (odd)—*r* only
Row 3 also produces three blocks of color, each color the opposite of the analogous block in Row 2.
At this point, you have four choices.

1. Continue the same pattern by spranging the next rows in regular twists only. Since the regular twist always brings up the color that is down, the blocks will change color every row.
2. Bring up all of one color across the row by spranging a full twist on the threads you gave a full twist before. In this case, you would sprang:
Row 4 (even)—10 *r*, 10 *f*, 10 *r*
3. Sprang two rows of Z twists. This automatically repeats the pattern in reverse.
4. Make a new pattern, using the full twist to bring up the desired colors. For example:
Row 4 (even)—6 *r*, 6 *f*, 6 *r*, 6 *f*, 6 *r*
Five blocks of color are formed.
Row 5 (odd)—*r* only
Five blocks of the opposite colors are formed.

As you may have noticed, a row of regular twists is placed between every pattern row. All pattern rows must be even or all must be odd. If you make two pattern rows one after the other, you will begin to form twists in which both threads are the same color. These twists can be used very effectively, as described in the following section on solid-color twists. Read on!

SOLID-COLOR TWISTS

The twists used to make blocks of color, or mixed-color twists, were each made of two colors. When each twist uses only one color, it is called a solid-color twist. The solid-color pattern begins forming at the point where you change from regular twists to full twists or from full twists to regular twists. We will refer to this as the point of change (see fig. 13-2).

Of course, when you sprang blocks of color, you have points of change. At each of these points, a solid-color twist is formed.

Fig. 13-4. Solid-color pattern. Alternating warp colors and full twists can produce varied areas of color.

However, a full pattern of solid-color twists does not appear unless the succeeding rows are spranged in full twists, not regular twists. The reason you must use full twists to obtain a pattern of solid-color twists will become apparent shortly.

Look at a point of change. The last upper thread on the right next to the point of change is the same color as the first lower thread to the left of the point of change, and

these are the two threads that will be twisted in the next row, producing a solid-color twist. After spranging the pattern row, all succeeding rows are spranged in full twists, so that the upper thread on the right and the lower thread on the left of the point of change are always the same color. The full twists always add two more threads to the section of solid-color twists. Therefore the solid-color pattern grows in a V (see fig. 13-1).

Solid-color twists are designated as *sc*. Mixed-color twists are designated as *m*. Remember that a full twist cannot be spranged on the first or last twists of a row. Since full twists take up more warp than regular twists, the edges of your piece will be rather loose, but not enough to affect its appearance. In the following example, there is one point of change occurring in Row 2 between the 15 regular and 14 full twists. In Row 3, the first solid-color twist appears at this point of change. Each row thereafter adds one solid color twist in the center.

You can control the color of the solid-color twists. The solid-color twists will always be the same color as the color you brought forward before spranging the first row. All the examples of solid-color patterns below show the pattern row as 15 *r*, 14 *f*, 1 *r*, with the full twists on the left of the piece. If you change the pattern row to 1 *r*, 14 *f*, 15 *r*, with the full twists on the right of the piece, the solid-color twists will be the other color. You will find that the upper threads to the right of the point of change are always the same color as the solid-color twists will be.

Row 1 (odd)—*r* only
All upper threads are the same color.
Row 2 (even)—15 *r*, 14 *f*, 1 *r*
Two blocks of color; all are mixed-color twists.
Row 3 (odd)—*f* only
The result is 14 *m*, 1 *sc*, 14 *m*. Did you

remember that full twists cannot be spranged on the first and last twists of the row?
Row 4 (even)—*f* only
The result is 1 *m*, 1 *sc*, 12 *m*, 2 *sc*, 12 *m*, 1 *sc*, 1 *m*.
Row 5 (odd)—*f* only
The result is 1 *m*, 1 *sc*, 11 *m*, 3 *sc*, 11 *m*, 1 *sc*, 1 *m*.
Row 6 (even)—*f* only
The result is 1 *m*, 2 *sc*, 10 *m*, 4 *sc*, 10 *m*, 2 *sc*, 1 *m*.

As the V-pattern of one color forms in the center of the sprang, the warp threads of the opposite color form solid-color twists at the right and left edges of the piece. Since a full twist is never spranged on the first or last twists, there are two more points of change— that between the first twist of the row and the twist to its left and that between the last twist of the row and the twist to its right. A section of solid-color twists, different in color from the center solid-color twists, forms at these points. One solid-color twist is added on each side in every other row. Continue the V-pattern far enough, and there will be no mixed twists left. At that point, the V inverts itself and begins to make a diamond pattern (see figure 13-1).

However, you can begin decreasing at any point you wish. When increasing the solid-color area, the upper thread to the right and the lower thread to the left of the point of change are of the same color as the solid-color twists; to decrease, these two threads must be the opposite color. A row of regular twists will change the color pattern to accomplish this. Sprang Rows 1 through 4 as you did to increase. Then sprang Row 5 in regular twists. There are three solid twists in Row 5. Sprang all succeeding rows in full twists only. Row 6 will have two solid-color twists, Row 7 one, and Row 8 none.

Fig. 13-5. Belts, various wool yarns, Mary Reddy. In the belt with the metal buckle, the full twist produces solid-color areas. In the belt with the wrapped buckle, full twists are combined with rows of S and Z twists.

Moving solid-color twists vertically and diagonally

By making only one point of change and continuing all subsequent rows in the full twist, you have been able to make a V and then a diamond of solid-color twists, as the color pattern moves to the left and right at the same time. You also have the choice of moving the pattern to the left only, to the right only, or straight up. Directions for each of these choices are given below. For the sake of simplicity, the first three rows will always be the same as before, and each pattern consists of only two or three solid-color twists. Of course, once you have mastered the different methods, you can make your own patterns, using one method or combining them. Again, a warp of 60 threads is used.

The key to moving the pattern to the left is the upper thread to the right of the solid-color area and the lower thread to the left. As long as these two threads are the same color as the solid-color twists, the solid-color pattern will grow to the right and left. However, if the upper thread to the right is the opposite color, the pattern will not be able to grow to the right. Instead, it will move only to the left. To bring the opposite color to the right of the solid-color pattern, sprang all of the threads on the right in regular twists. In the pattern below, this is done in Row 4. You could sprang only the two threads to the right of the solid-color twists as a regular twist and all of the other threads on the right as full twists. However, then you would have an additional point of change between the first group of full twists and the regular twist.

Row 1 (odd)—*r* only
All upper threads are the same color.
Row 2 (even)—15 *r*, 14 *f*, 1 *r*
Two blocks of color; all are mixed-color twists.
Row 3 (odd)—*f* only
The result is 14 *m*, 1 *sc*, 14 *m*.
Row 4 (even)—14 *r*, 15 *f*, 1 *r*
The result is 1 *m*, 1 *sc*, 12 *m*, 2 *sc*, 12 *m*, 1 *sc*, 1 *m*.
Row 5 (odd)—*f* only
The result is 14 *m*, 2 *sc*, 11 *m*, 1 *sc*, 1 *m*.
Continue the pattern using only full twists.

An interesting effect can be produced by moving only one solid-color twist to the left instead of two, as above. To achieve this, sprang Row 3 as follows, and all succeeding twists as full twists.

Row 3 (odd)—14 *r*, 14 *f*, 1 *r*
The one solid-color twist will continue moving to the left in this variation.

To move the pattern to the right, the lower thread to the left of the solid-color twists should be of the alternate color. Then, the pattern cannot grow to the left. To achieve this, sprang all of the threads to the left of the solid-color section in regular twists. In the pattern below this is done in Row 4.

Rows 1—3 (odd, even, odd)—same as above
Row 4 (even)—1 *r*, 15 *f*, 14 *r*
The result is 1 *m*, 1 *sc*, 12 *m*, 2 *sc*, 12 *m*, 1 *sc*, 1 *m*.
Row 5 (odd)—*f* only
The result is 1 *m*, 1 *sc*, 11 *m*, 2 *sc*, 14 *m*.
Continue the pattern with full twists in each succeeding row.

To move the pattern vertically, sprang almost in the same manner as you did when making block patterns of mixed-color twists. The full twist is used to achieve the basic pattern, and the regular twist, instead of the full twist used previously, is used to continue the pattern straight up. The row of regular twists always brings up the color that was down in the preceding row. Therefore, in one row, the upper thread lying to the right and the lower thread to the left of the solid-color section are the same color as the solid-color twists, so the pattern increases by one twist. In the next row, the upper thread to the right and the lower thread to the left of the solid-color twists are the opposite color, decreasing the solid-color twists by one. As long as the regular twist is used, the pattern increases by one twist and decreases by one in alternate rows.

Rows 1--3 (odd, even, odd)—same as above
Row 4 (even)—*f* only
The result is 1 *m*, 1 *sc*, 12 *m*, 2 *sc*, 12 *m*, 1 *sc*, 1 *m*.
Row 5 (odd)—*r* only
This continues the pattern with 1 *m*, 1 *sc*,

11 *m*, 3 *sc*, 11 *m*, 1 *sc*, 1 *m*.
Row 6 (even)—*r* only
This continues the pattern with 1 *m*, 1 *sc*,
12 *m*, 2 *sc*, 12 *m*, 1 *sc*, 1 *m*.
Notice that Row 4 is just like Row 6.
Rows 5 and 7 will also be identical. Row 8
will be like Rows 4 and 6.

Fig. 13-6. Hanging, synthetic raffia, Lisa Ridenour. A free use of full twists with S and Z twists makes the most of contrasting colors.

14 Finishing and Special Effects

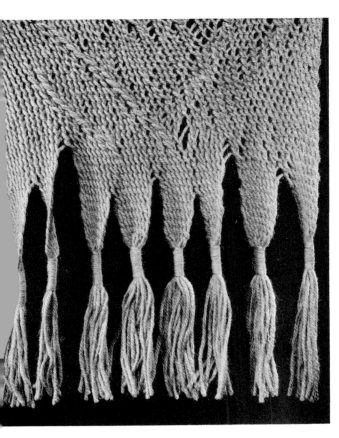

Fig. 14-1. Detail of Fig. 9-2. To create the fringe, slits in the center of the piece were started but not closed. The fringes were wrapped tightly *before* the warp was cut.

Just as a painting deserves a good frame, your sprang also deserves enough care in finishing to truly enhance the work. Blocking or pressing the piece will retain the desired shape and securing the ends of the warp and the closing thread will make its appearance neater. The care taken in finishing your sprang will make all the rest of your work worthwhile.

BLOCKING

Before you take the piece off the dowels, thread a string through the loops. It is not absolutely necessary to do this, as the sprang will not unravel if you don't. However, it holds the loops in order so they will all lie in the same direction when pressed.

After removing the dowels, stretch the sprang out flat to the desired length, width, and shape. An ironing board or other large padded board can be used. The shape can be secured by pinning the sides to the board or by using Velcro, the flocked tape often used in belt and skirt fastenings. If you use pins, place them close together to prevent the sprang from drawing in between the pins. Velcro must be pinned down also but only at the ends and a few places in between. Velcro is really the best answer although it is somewhat expensive.

It is easiest to shape and block your piece if you secure the top and bottom first, and then pull out from the center to the desired width. After that, secure the sides one at a time.

Hold a steam iron just above the piece, and let the steam soak in. Go over the whole piece several times. If you use a dampened pressing cloth, you can place the iron directly on the cloth, but only use a very light touch. Pressing hard flattens the twists. Transparent pressing cloths are sold that let you see through to the sprang so that you will know if the pins or Velcro need readjustment. Instead of steaming, you can sprinkle or sponge the piece with cold water and let it dry.

Be sure not to move the sprang until it is dry. This may take several hours or overnight. Certainly, you will be anxious to finish your piece, but moving the sprang while it is still damp ruins all of your blocking work.

If you have not used a continuous warp, you may block the piece right in the frame. Stretch the sprang to the desired width, and secure the edges to the frame with stretch cords at many points. To prevent drawing in between the stretch cords, you could thread a 1/8-inch dowel through the twists at the sides. Then you need to use only a few stretch cords on either side. Steam as usual and let dry.

If the piece does not have to be stretched much, there may be no need to secure the edges to the ironing board or the frame. Simply steam the piece and let it dry.

SECURING THE CLOSING THREAD

The closing thread simply can be tied off at the edges or it can be used in finishing the piece. Whichever method you use, be sure to block the sprang first to determine the width.

To tie the closing thread off at each edge, lay out the blocked sprang on a flat surface so you will be sure to keep the blocked width. If the closing row was even, tie the ends of the closing thread in a knot around the outside thread. If the closing row was odd, knot around the two outside threads. Place a dab of clear glue on each knot and make another knot over the first. When the glue is dry, the knots are very secure and you can cut the ends off close to the knots.

The long ends of the closing thread can also become useful parts of the finished work. The ends can be used to sew together the sides of pillows and purses. Knot the ends at the edges first. Fold the sprang in half, with the closing thread at the bottom. Lash the closing thread ends through the outer twists, which will sew the sides of the piece together, and secure the ends at the top of the piece.

If you are working on a hanging, you might simply lead the closing-thread ends up the outside twists of the sprang and secure them at the top of the frame or on the dowel from which the sprang is hanging. Or, for example, the closing thread in a scarf could be run through the outside twists and knotted into the last loop. If you have spranged several sections, the closing threads can run both up and down the edges of the sprang.

VARIATIONS ON CLOSINGS

The closing can be more than just a thread to hold the sprang together. It might become a decoration in itself or blend harmoniously into the design of the whole sprang.

Looping

A looped closing can be used where you need a particularly strong and secure closing, such as in a purse or pillow. Since looping spreads out the sprang at the closing, it can be utilized to shape your sprang, as in Figures 14–2 and 14–3.

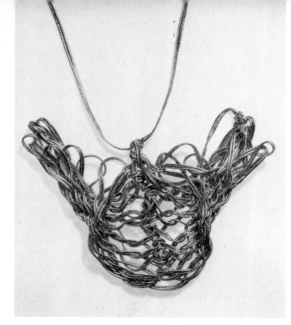

Fig. 14-2. Necklace, gold soutache, Hella Skowronski. The looped closing holds the shape, and one side is folded up to the center, where it is secured.

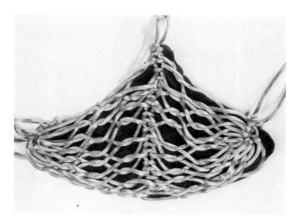

Fig. 14-3. Detail of Figure 4-2. A looped closing, done on the back, was used to advantage for shaping.

When spranging, you have always worked from right to left. However, a looped closing is worked from left to right. Follow the steps below.

1. Sprang the last row as even.
2. Leave approximately two inches unspranged in the center of the warp. There is a great deal of take-up in looping. You should allow for this take-up when calculating the length of the warp.
3. Loosen the tension of the warp.
4. Using a crochet hook, pull the first upper thread on the left side under the first lower thread on the left (figs. 14–4 and 14–5).

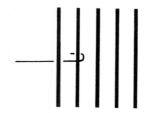

Fig. 14-4. Looped closing, step one. Note that looping starts from the left.

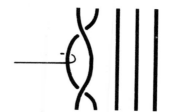

Fig. 14-5. Completing the first loop.

5. Bring the crochet hook over the first lower thread on the left (fig. 14–6).

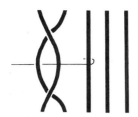

Fig. 14-6. Beginning the second loop.

6. Pull the next lower thread, which is the third thread, through the loop made (fig. 14-7).

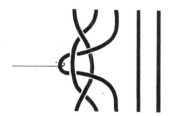

Fig. 14-7. Completing the second loop.

7. Pick up the next upper thread, which is the fourth thread, and pull it through the loop just made (fig. 14-8).

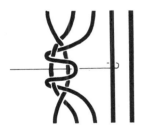

Fig. 14-8. Beginning the third loop.

8. Pull each succeeding thread through the last loop made. Continue to the end of the row (fig. 14-9).

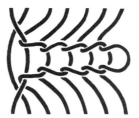

Fig. 14-9. Looped closing, completed.

A loop will remain on the right side. This must be secured by pulling a piece of yarn or thread through the last loop and then tying the last two warp threads together.

You do not have to loop all of the threads. If you loop only the upper threads, the lower threads will float behind. Or you could loop the upper threads and then turn the loom over and loop the lower threads separately.

Looping spreads the sprang out and makes a somewhat stiffer closing. Although this can be used decoratively, you can use looping for strength only. Simply do your looping on the back side of the sprang, and it will not show. If you use a continuous warp or weaving loom, you will have to make the looped closing on the working side of the piece. If you don't want the looped closing to show, use the back of the piece for the front. Some excellent examples of looped closings are shown in Figures 14–10 and 14–11.

Fig. 14-10. Hanging, wool, Lisa Ridenour. Looped closings on a piece in three sections were worked at the back of the sprang.

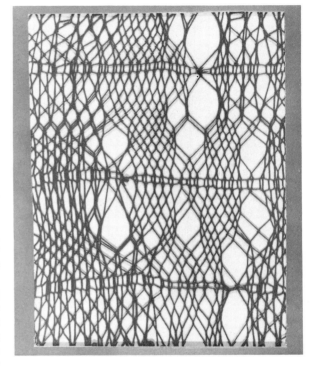

Fig. 14-11. Detail of a looped closing that has been left open enough for an additional thread to be stitched in the space created.

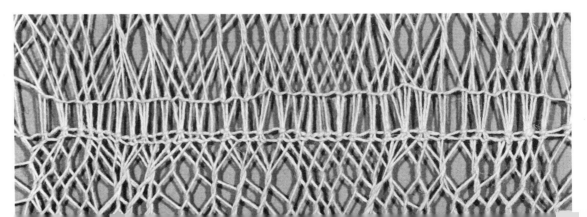

Doubles, trebles, and slits

A very decorative way to close is with doubles or trebles. The closing row simply may be spranged 2/2 or 3/3. However, to give a different effect, you can sprang the closing so that the closing thread goes through only one upper and one lower thread of each double or treble. For a closing using doubles, like that in Figure 14–12, follow the steps below.

1. Sprang the row before the closing in doubles, but begin and end it 1/1.
2. Sprang the closing row in doubles. All of the twists, including the first and last, are 2/2.

The same method is used with trebles.

1. Sprang the row before the closing in trebles. Either begin the row 1/1 and end it 2/2 or begin 2/2 and end 1/1.
2. Sprang all of the twists in the closing row, including the first and last, 3/3.

Fig. 14-12. Detail of hanging by Marney Chapman on page 6. The closing, using doubles, employs a thread that runs through only one upper and one lower thread of each double twist.

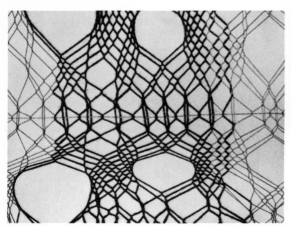

Try spranging the closing in such a way as to leave unclosed slits. The closing thread then runs through the center of the slits, giving the middle area of the piece a very open appearance.

Unusual closing threads

The thread used to close does not have to be exactly like the rest of your warp. Clear nylon thread takes on the color of the warp yarns, so that the thread itself becomes invisible. If your warp yarn is bulkier than you want for the closing, untwist it and use only one strand for the closing. Be sure to test the resulting single ply for strength, as it might break easily. Try closing with something other than just yarn—a pipe cleaner covered with yarn, beads strung on yarn, leather, brass tubes, or wood. All make interesting closings. Can you think of more?

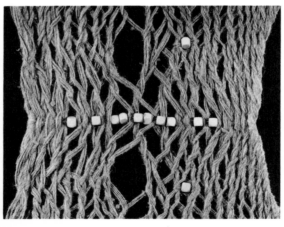

Fig. 14-13. Detail of Figure 6-5 shows closing with beads strung on the closing thread.

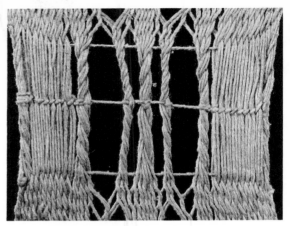

Fig. 14-14. Detail of Figure 5-1 shows a knotted closing. The other two threads are not the actual closing but serve to hold the twists in place.

MOUNTING A HANGING

The method used to hang or frame your piece should complement the structure, texture, and color of the sprang itself. Is your sprang light and delicate? Then a thin frame or dowel for hanging may be best. Did you use heavy yarns? A heavier structure is needed to support such a hanging, both practically and aesthetically. Did you use more than one color in your warp? You could emphasize one of these colors by painting the frame or dowel the same color. Is the design of your sprang striking and simple? Perhaps a modern chrome frame would suit such a hanging. Be careful, though, not to detract from the sprang itself by overdoing the framing.

Free-hanging sprang

The first step in hanging is preparing the dowel or other support from which the piece will hang. If it is wood, cut, sand, and paint

Fig. 14-15. Hanging, wool, Carol Bodily. An unusual framing uses differently sized pieces on the sides, placed so that the sprang is smaller at the top.

or stain the dowel or stick. If metal, simply have the rod cut to your specifications and the ends filed. When finished, put the support through the top loops of the sprang.

To maintain the width of the piece, the left and right edges must be fastened to the dowel. The simplest way to do this is with glue. First tie the long top ends at the beginning and ending of the warp around the dowel and glue them in place. Then tie the two loose ends together to form the hanger. Either one long end can be tied to the beginning of the other end, right at the dowel, or the two ends can be joined so they form a longer hanger. If you want the bottom of the sprang weighted, place a second dowel through the lower loops, and glue the outer edge loops of the sprang to the dowel.

An even more secure method of maintaining the width is achieved by drilling two holes in the dowel, one at each end. Then you can pull the end of each slipknot through itself, making a second knot at each edge. Thread the long ends through the holes in the dowel. Be sure the knots you made are large enough not to slip back through the holes.

You can then join the long ends to make a hanger, put a dowel through the bottom loops for weight, and glue the outer loops to the dowel.

If you do not want to use the long ends for hanging, tie them around the dowel, glue them, and try to keep the knots at the back of the dowel, out of sight. Then cut off the long ends next to the knots, and attach a rope for hanging to the ends of the dowel with a hitch. Place the rope inside the outer loops to maintain the width.

Framed sprang

A sprang can be framed with the loops showing or covered. If they do not show, the sprang looks more picture-frame finished, but on the other hand the loops can be very decorative in themselves. Choose the method best for your particular piece.

It is easiest to frame a hanging and leave the loops showing, as in Figure 14–16. To do this, place the top and bottom pieces of the frame through the loops. Secure the side pieces of the frame to the top and bottom with glue and picture-frame nails. Use the long ends to lash the sides of the sprang to the sides of the frame. When you made the warp, you left long ends of four to five times the length of the warp. Use these long ends to lash the sides of the sprang to the sides of the frame, so that the edges are straight. Use your own judgment to determine how often to insert the lashing. For heavy yarns this would be about every row and for fine yarns about every other row.

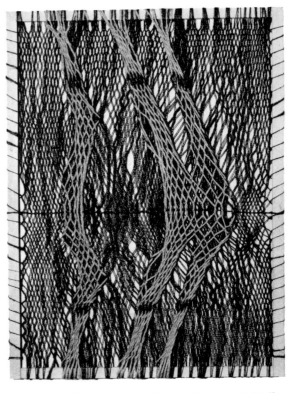

Fig. 14-16. Hanging, rayon slub and rug wool, Hella Skowronski. The exposed loops are very decorative in this framing. The hanging is an example of an advanced sprang technique—semi-double sprang. An overlay of rug yarn was warped after the background warp, and in some areas it was spranged separately, although the two were always interlocked at the edges. (Collection of Mrs. Roy O. Hansen.)

If you want to cover the loops, you must from the beginning warp the sprang on thin, flat sticks instead of dowels. Then, when you are finished with your piece, attach the top and bottom sticks to side sticks. Use the long ends to lash the sprang to the sticks at the sides. When the sprang is secured, cover the stick frame with an outer frame, which will hide the loops and lashings.

Permanent frame

The frame loom on which you warp and sprang can also be the frame for hanging. This idea originated with Peter Collingwood, an English weaver. Obviously, it is easier to finish a hanging when the hanging is already on the frame. However, special attention must be paid to the strength and appearance of the frame before you warp. Figure 14–17 shows a sprang in progress on such a frame.

First you must make or buy a four-sided frame, a few inches longer than the intended length of your sprang. Make sure the frame is strong. Then, make a piece of wood to match the frame, long enough to fit snugly inside the width of the frame (A). When finished, this piece will be the bottom of the frame, glued and nailed to the sides. But do not nail it in yet.

Next, paint or stain the frame and the extra piece. When they are dry, tie the extra piece inside the frame by fastening tension release cords from it to the bottom of the frame (B). Leave enough room between the extra piece and the bottom of the frame for a ball of yarn to pass through. Warp around the extra piece and the top of the frame, leaving long ends where the warp begins and ends (C). These ends should be four to five times the length of the warp. Sprang as usual, and, as you sprang, lash stretch cords through the outside twists to the sides of the frame. This ensures that the width of the piece will fit the frame.

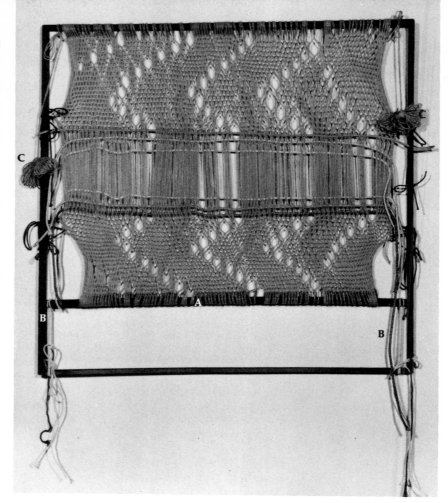

Fig. 14-17. Permanent frame, showing extra piece that will become the bottom of the frame (A), tension release cords to fasten the extra piece (B), and long ends where the warp begins and ends (C). When finished spranging, the lower portion of the frame is cut off below the dowel holding the bottom loops. The completed piece is shown in Figure 10-13.

As usual, close the center when you have reached the middle.

When you have finished spranging, finish the frame. Glue and nail the ends of the extra piece (A) to the frame, thus securing it in place. You can now remove the tension release cords (B). Cut off the bottom of the frame directly below the extra piece, and paint or stain the cut ends. The extra piece is now the bottom of the frame. At the top, you tied the beginning and ending of the warp with knots and slipknots. Pull the end of the slipknot through, so as to make a second knot. Lace the long ends from the top around the sides of the frame and through the outer twists of the sprang, replacing the stretch cords.

Finish by securing the ends for lacing at the bottom behind the frame. Make a knot, place a dab of glue on it and then make another knot. Cut off the free end. Tie the closing thread to the sides of the frame, making knots, as above, in the back.

SPECIAL EFFECTS

There are many ways to personalize your sprang or use it in an unusual manner. Surface decoration can be added—sew shells or beads into slits or elaborate with stitchery. Explore the possibilities of combining other media with sprang. The more you sprang, the more you will find methods of bringing your personal style to your work. Here are a few suggestions for you to try.

Fig. 14-18. Necklace, braided nylon fishline, tensolite, and glass beads, Virginia Harvey. The frame for this necklace, only 2½ inches square, was cut from a plastic container and wrapped after the sprang was worked. It was closed with a row of glass beads.

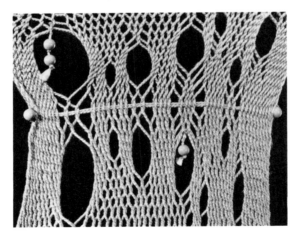

Fig. 14-19. Beads embellish the closing as well as the slits in this detail from a piece by Nancy Dice.

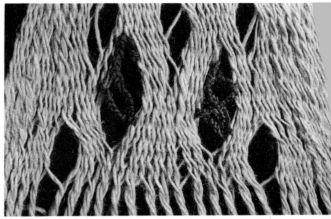

Fig. 14-20. Slits can be enhanced by crocheting.

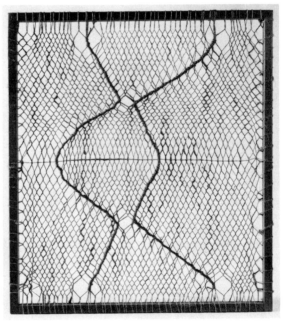

Fig. 14-21. Hanging, slub rayon, Sheila Demetre. A simple sprang is made visually interesting by a silhouette of stitchery.

Fig. 14-22. Hanging, mohair loop and painted background, Marney Chapman. Combining two art media can produce exciting results.

Fig. 14-23. Detail of cape shown in color on page 12. The sprang is joined to leather with a chain stitch that is echoed in finishing details.

Two pieces out of one

What you sprang on the bottom produces a mirror effect on the top, and your sprang can be cut into two pieces, one in S twists, the other in Z twists. This is very effective for side-by-side wall hangings or matching pillows or the front and back of a simple squared-off vest. The two pieces can also be made to look quite different from each other by the way in which they are finished.

Of course, sprang cannot simply be cut in the center without taking some precautions against unraveling, but these preventative measures can become very beautiful parts of the design. The hangings in Figures 9–2 and 9–3 are ideal examples of this. Slits were spranged but never closed. The groups of twists in between the slits were then wrapped securely with yarn while the sprang was still on tension on the loom. Only then was the sprang cut, leaving a fringe.

Another method of securing the sprang is to knot the cut ends while the sprang is still on tension on the loom. Be sure *not* to cut the whole sprang before you make the knots. Leave enough thread untwisted in the center of the warp to give you something to hang onto when you knot. Cut one twist at a time, knotting one lower thread with one upper thread. To keep even tension as you cut, cut a twist on the left, then one on the right, until the last twist cut is the one in the center.

Making use of loops

If you wish to give a firm edge to your sprang, you can crochet through the loops. Not only is this practical in helping the piece hold its shape, but it also can be very decorative.

If you are making a handbag, thread a rope or cord through the loops at the top and bottom and you will have a drawstring. Follow the instructions on page 82 for sewing up the sides of a pillow, and you will quickly have a sprang bag. String bags like this are often used by French women for marketing.

The loops can be used to connect one piece of sprang to another. How about a sprang afghan? Fascinating projects for children may be developed using this method, as the frame loom can be quite small and each piece very simple in structure. Try to use color to full advantage when combining more than one piece. The easiest way to attach one piece to another is by threading a string or piece of yarn through the loops. Pick up one loop from each piece alternately. To attach two pieces at the sides, lace string or yarn through the outer twists of each piece, lashing the two together.

Crocheting the pieces together provides a stronger attachment. The crocheting may even become a part of the design of the finished piece. With either method, it is best to warp onto thin dowels so that the loops at the bottom and top will be small.

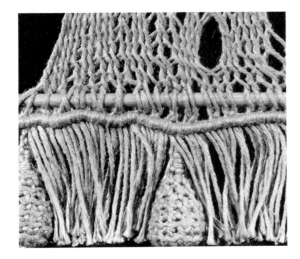

Fig. 14-24. Detail of fringe in Figure 5-1. The fringe consists of a finishing row of macramé, loose ends, and fishing weights covered with crochet.

Shaped sprang

One of the beauties of sprang is that it does not have to be square and flat. There are many ways in which it can be shaped. Fanciful three-dimensional hangings and mobiles can be created simply by stretching the sprang and stringing wire through the loops and twists on the edges.

Another way to shape your piece is by making use of the turning effect produced when S and Z twists are spranged. At the

Fig. 14-25. Vest, wool, Aves Pickering. Done on a shaped warp, the front was spranged in one piece with a dowel for the armholes, one for the neck opening, and a third for the shoulders.

Fig. 14-26. The back of the vest used only two dowels, one for the armholes and one for the neckline. Shoulder straps constructed on the front piece were joined to the back later.

point between a row of S and a row of Z, the piece tends to twist in one direction or the other rather than lying flat.

The warp itself does not have to be made in a square or rectangular form. The vest shown in Figures 14–25 and 14–26 was warped to form armholes and shoulder straps. A shaped warp employs warp threads of different lengths. For each length of warp thread, there must be a top and bottom dowel (fig. 14–27). The vest was formed with one dowel for all of the loops at the bottom. Three dowels were used for the top: the highest for the shoulder straps, the next for the neckline, and the third for the armholes, where the warp length was shortest.

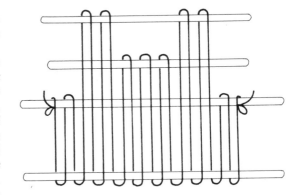

Fig. 14-27. A shaped warp. With careful preplanning you can sprang many items on shaped warps. The arrangement shown here is for the vest front in Figure 14-25.

15 For Weavers Only

Those of you who weave have another fascinating way to put sprang to work. A loom lends itself easily to sprang, and just as when you weave you can sprang pieces of any length. Depending on the width of your loom, you will be able to make wider-than-usual sprangs as well.

Fig. 15-1. Hanging, weaving and sprang, Sylvia Tacker. This contains examples of sprang within weaving and sprang on a woven background.

Fig. 15-2. Detail of Figure 15-1.

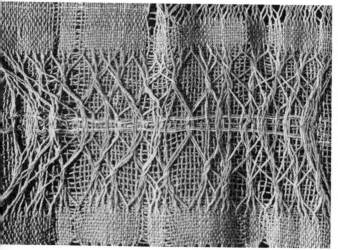

The loom also enables you to combine weaving with sprang. A woven fabric interspersed with sprang is strikingly attractive because of the complex visual interplay of thread patterns. The sprang can also be worked right over the weave for a layered effect. If you are familiar with Tarascan lace, you already know something of sprang, since the same technique is used for doubles and singles.

If you intend to sprang without weaving, beam the loom using either a reed or a raddle, as described below. The heddles are not used. If you intend to combine weaving and sprang, dress the loom just as you do for weaving.

Since you are already familiar with the terms and operations of weaving, our explanations are given only when a loom set-up technique is modified for sprang.

Fig. 15-3. Hanging, Soumak weaving and sprang, Kit Chapman. Two textile techniques, done in different qualities of yarn, are combined to mutual advantage.

Fig. 15-4. Detail of Figure 15-3.

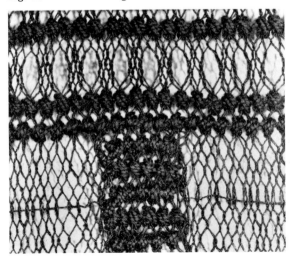

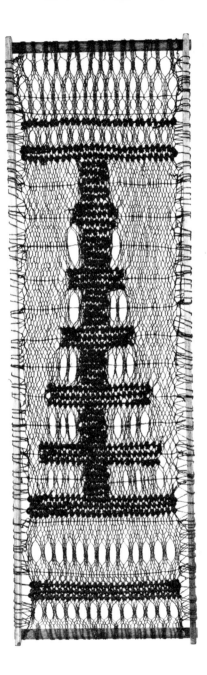

SPRANG ONLY

Warping

Make your warp chain as usual, tying on and off at the opposite end from the cross. There are just a few minor differences when preparing a warp for spranging.

At the starting point, tie on with a knot and slipknot, leaving a long end. After warping as many threads as you want, be sure to tie off with a knot and slipknot at the same place you started. Again, leave a long end. The long ends will later be tied to the stick or rod attached to the warp beam, and in the completed sprang will be used for finishing. Tying on and off at the same place produces an even number of warp threads so that you will have an equal number of upper and lower threads.

Tie the cross as you normally do, but also secure the loops at each end of the warp. This keeps the warp even and makes it easy to slip the loops over the stick or rod on the loom.

Using a reed for spreading

Spread the warp in the reed to the desired width. If you don't mind losing the loops on one end of the sprang, beam as usual. Cut the warp loops, remove the reed, and tie the cut ends to the stick on the cloth beam.

If you want to keep the loops on both ends of the piece, use the following method so that you will be able to remove the reed. The difference in spreading the warp for spranging is that the chain is placed in back of the reed and in back of the loom. The lease sticks are also in back of the reed. Sley the warp loops from the back of the reed to the front. Then put a string through the loops and tie the loops tightly together to keep your warp in order.

Pull the warp through the reed to the front. If your warp is very long, you probably will have to rechain as you pull. Pull the warp far enough so the loops in the back of the loom can be slipped over the warp stick. Tie the long ends to the warp stick. Now that the warp is in front of the loom, beam as usual. Remove the reed and slip the loops over the stick attached to the cloth beam.

The first thread on the right side must be up for spranging. Put the shed stick into the shed of the lease stick on which this first thread is up. Remove both lease sticks.

Using a raddle for spreading

Beam the loom as you normally would to weave. Spread the warp in the raddle with the lease sticks in front of the raddle. Wind the warp onto the warp beam. Slip the loops in the front of the loom over the stick attached to the cloth beam. The raddle can be left in the back of the loom to keep the warp spread.

Spranging on the loom

Spranging is done exactly the same way on a weaving loom as on a frame loom. Before beginning, insert a shed stick so that the first thread on the right is up. Sprang the warp in sections, using a stop cord, which is tied to the sides of the loom. The stop cord should be placed within a comfortable reaching distance. Tie the stretch cords to the sides of the loom, wherever it is convenient. If you used a raddle and left it in the back of the loom to keep the warp spread, the raddle must be removed to sprang the last section.

WEAVING AND SPRANG COMBINED

Make your warp and dress the loom as you normally would in preparation for weaving. The reed is left in and the ends are threaded through the heddles.

Fig. 15-5. Shawl, weaving and sprang, Sylvia Tacker. Wool and mohair, woven in a four-harness overshot, is spranged with singles and slits.

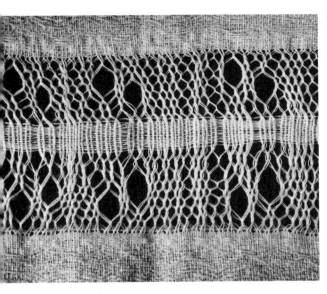

Fig. 15-6. Detail of shawl's sprang shows closing woven with a needle.

Fig. 15-7. Hostess skirt, weaving and sprang, Aves Pickering. A wide area of sprang produces an elegant garment. (A detail of the sprang is shown in Figure 6-1.)

Spranging with weaving

The hostess skirt in Figure 15–7 is a beautiful example of using sprang with weaving. The sprang turns a simple piece of fabric into an elegantly fashioned garment.

Weave as much length as desired. When ready to begin a section of sprang, place a stop cord in front of the reed. Insert the shed stick so that the first thread on the right is up. Sprang the section and close the center.

Wind the warp forward. If you wish to continue to sprang, move the stop cord in front of the reed again and sprang Section 2. If you do not wish to continue the sprang, simply resume weaving.

Overlay of sprang

An overlay is sprang worked on top of a woven background. You will find that sprang takes up more than weaving. If your overlay section is long, you will need to make two warp chains, the sprang chain longer than the other. Weave as much length as desired. To begin the overlay section, weave the length of the overlay, using only two harnesses, assuming you are using a four-harness loom. The other two harnesses hold the threads that will be spranged. Keep these up while weaving.

Let the sprang harnesses down or keep them up if more convenient. Insert the stop cord and shed stick and sprang the length of the overlay. The overlay section may be as long as you wish. However, only weave the area between the breast beam and the reed before spranging the top threads. Then you can roll the warp forward and continue by weaving with two harnesses again and then spranging the second section. If you do not wish to continue the overlay, remove the stop cord and begin weaving again.

Closings

You will discover some interesting closings when you sprang overlays. The pillow in Figure 15–8 and the hanging in Figure 15–2 show two methods you might try.

In the pillow, the sprang is closed with a strong but fine thread sewn right into the weaving. This not only closes the sprang but tacks the overlay down, a particularly good idea in an object handled as often as a pillow.

The closing shown in the hanging is a regular one, which floats on top of the weaving. However, it is extended to the outside edges of the weaving, at which point it is stitched in. This not only makes a secure closing but also provides an extra focal point in the work.

Fig. 15-8. Pillow cover, weaving and sprang, Aves Pickering. Rayon and wool yarns were warped alternately. The wool was brought up for the sprang.

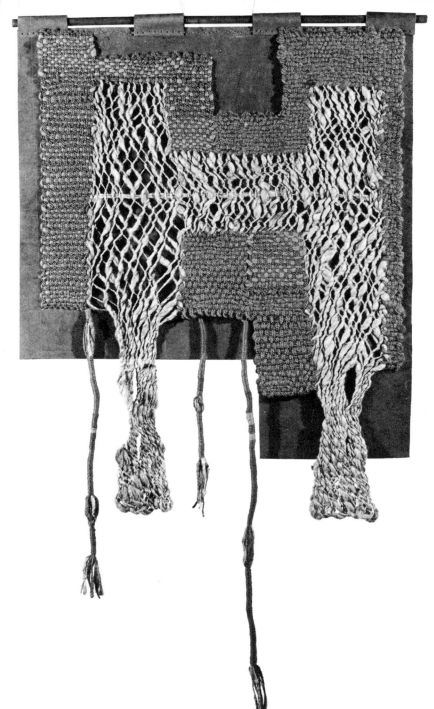

Fig. 15-9. *Twisted Flappy Bird*, weaving and sprang on leather background, by Luana Severs. The scaffold weaving and sprang are worked into a unified design with wrapped fringes for a finishing touch.

Conclusion

Writing this book has been a delightful process of discovery for us. There is so much we have learned, yet so much still to be learned. We hope that you will find this book merely a starting point in your exploration of sprang.

Part of our enjoyment has been in sharing the techniques of sprang with others, for we feel that sprang should be and will be enjoyed by many people once they have been introduced to it. Many weavers and designers, who have just caught glimpses of sprang here and there, are already asking to know more about it. And those who are spranging now are finding it a fascinating and versatile craft.

With the great interest in handcrafts at this time among amateurs as well as professionals, sprang is sure to find its place. The equipment is inexpensive, the techniques are easy to learn, and the results are rewarding. As one of the many people who have come to sprang, you now have the opportunity to discover more techniques for yourself by expanding on what you have already learned. Play with new ways to shape your work into "sprang sculptures." Look for opportunities to use sprang in clothing. Those of you who have done double weaving will want to try double sprang.

Due to space, we have not been able to touch on every aspect of sprang. There is more to be done and discoveries yet to be made. If your imagination has been teased, join us in exploring this exciting and rewarding craft.

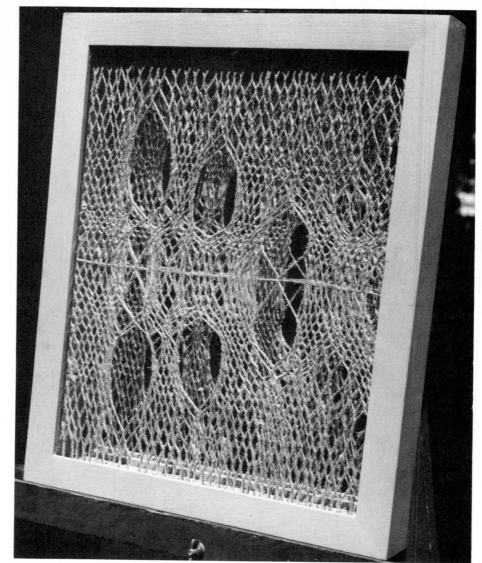

Mirrored wall hanging, fine linen, Hella Skowronski. A simple design of singles and slits is striking when seen twice, the mirror reflecting the sprang. Two strands of fine linen were warped as one. (Photo by Paul Gilmore.)

Glossary

closing row—the last row of a sprang, usually close to the center of the warp, which secures the twists.

continuous warp—a method of making a long warp; the warp begins and ends on the same movable dowel.

diagonal slits—an opening formed when one slit is closed and a new one is made to the right or left of it in the same row.

double twist—a twist in which two lower threads are picked up and two upper threads are pushed down; 2/2.

drawing-in—the tendency of the sprang to curve in towards the center.

even row—the row in which, when using singles on the edges, the first and last twists are spranged with one upper and one lower thread each.

frame loom—a square or rectangular form used to hold the warp.

full twist—two threads are twisted as in a regular twist and then twisted around themselves again.

looped closing—a method of closing the sprang; each thread is pulled through a loop made by the adjacent thread.

lower thread—the thread below the dowel, shed cord, or shed stick.

mixed-color twist—a twist in which the upper and lower threads are of different colors.

odd row—when using S-twist singles on edges, row which begins by picking up two lower threads and pushing down one upper thread and ends by picking up one lower thread and pushing down two upper threads. With Z twists, singles start two down, one up, and end two up, one down.

opening—formed at some points of change; slit.

overlay—a layer of sprang over a layer of sprang or weaving.

permanent frame loom—a frame loom which becomes the frame for a hanging.

pick-up stick—the short stick used to pick up the threads.

point of change—the place in a row where twists are changed from S to Z or from one twist to another.

S twist—a twist in which the lower thread is picked up and brought to the right before the upper thread is pushed down.

section—one segment of a sprang, having a top, a bottom, and a closing row, and followed or preceded by another section.

shaped warp—a warp that uses threads of different length to achieve a shape other than a square or rectangle.

shed—the space between the upper and lower threads.

shed cord—the cord placed in the shed to hold a row of twists.

shed stick—the stick holding open the shed of a row of twists just made.

single twist—a twist consisting of one upper and one lower thread; 1/1.

simple twist—a twist in which the two threads to be twisted are adjacent to each other with no thread between.

slit—an opening formed within a regular pattern.

solid-color twist—when using full twists, a twist in which the upper and lower threads are of the same color.

stop cord—the cord which stops the twist, ending a section and beginning a new one.

stop shed—the shed held by the stop cord.

stretch cords—strings tying the sprang to the frame to stretch the sprang to its full width while being worked.

take-up—shortening of the warp threads due to twisting.

tension-release cords—strings tying the dowels to the frame; used to adjust the tension on the warp.

transfer stick—the long stick to which the twists are transferred from the pick-up stick.

treble twist—a twist made up of three upper and three lower threads; 3/3.

two-row sequence—an odd row followed by an even row; must be used when spranging singles on the edges.

upper thread—the thread above the dowel, shed cord, or shed stick.

warp—the threads wound onto the loom.

warping—the process of winding the yarn onto the loom.

Z twist—a twist made when the upper thread is pushed down and to the right before the lower thread is brought up.

Bibliography

BOOKS

Allen, Helen Louise. *American and European Hand Weaving Revised*. Madison, Wisconsin: Democrat Printing Company, 1939.

Birrell, Verla. *The Textile Arts*. New York: Harper and Row, 1959.

Black, Mary E. *New Key to Weaving*. Milwaukee: The Bruce Publishing Co., 1957.

D'Harcourt, Raoul; ed., Grace G. Denny and Carolyn M. Osbourne; trans., Sadie Brown. *Textiles of Ancient Peru and Their Techniques*. Seattle: University of Washington Press, 1962.

Emery, Irene. *The Primary Structure of Fabrics*. Washington, D.C.: Textile Museum, 1966.

Hald, Margarethe. *Ancient Danish Textiles*. Copenhagen: Gyldendal, 1950.

Norbury, James and Agutter, Margaret. *Odham's Encyclopaedia of Knitting*. Long Acre, London: Odham's Press Ltd., 1957.

Van Reesema, Door E. *Egyptisch Vlechtwerk*. Amsterdam: V. Holkema and Warendorf's.

Wilson, Jean. *Weaving is Creative*. New York: Van Nostrand Reinhold, 1972.

ARTICLES

Collingwood, Peter. "A Sampler in Sprang," *Threads in Action*, Vol. 2, No. 2, Winter, 1970.

———. "Sprang, Revival of an Ancient Technique," *Handweaver and Craftsman*, Vol. 15, No. 2, Spring, 1964.

Harvey, Virginia. "Profile of Textile Craftsman, Hella Skowronski," *Threads in Action*, Vol. 2, No. 3, Spring, 1971.

———. "Sprang One," *Threads in Action*, Vol. 1, No. 4, 1969.

"Hella Skowronski Experiments with Sprang," *Handweaver and Craftsman*, Vol. 20, No. 1, Winter, 1969.

Lund, Jeannette. "Sprang," *Threads in Action*, Vol. 2, No. 1, Fall, 1970.

Index